MODERN WORLD LEADERS

Nicolas Sarkozy

MODERN WORLD LEADERS

Michelle Bachelet

Ban Ki-moon

Tony Blair

Gordon Brown

George W. Bush

Felipe Calderón

Hugo Chávez

Jacques Chirac

Hu Jintao

Hamid Karzai

Ali Khamenei

Kim Jong II

Thabo Mbeki

Angela Merkel

Hosni Mubarak

Pervez Musharraf

Ehud Olmert

Pope Benedict XVI

Pope John Paul II

Roh Moo Hyun

Vladimir Putin

Nicolas Sarkozy

The Saudi Royal Family

Ariel Sharon

Viktor Yushchenko

MODERN WORLD LEADERS

Nicolas Sarkozy

Dennis Abrams

CHELSEA HOUSE
PUBLISHERS

An imprint of Infobase Publishing

Nicolas Sarkozy

Copyright © 2009 by Infobase Publishing

All rights reserved. No part of this book may be reproduced or utilized in any form or by any means, electronic or mechanical, including photocopying, recording, or by any information storage or retrieval systems, without permission in writing from the publisher. For information, contact:

Chelsea House
An imprint of Infobase Publishing
132 West 31st Street
New York, NY 10001

Library of Congress Cataloging-in-Publication Data
Abrams, Dennis, 1960–
Nicolas Sarkozy / by Dennis Abrams.
   p. cm. — (Modern world leaders)
Includes bibliographical references and index.
ISBN 978-1-60413-081-2 (hardcover)
1. Sarkozy, Nicolas, 1955– 2. Presidents—France—Biography. 3. France—Politics and government—1995– I. Title.
DC433.A37 2009
944.084092—dc22
   [B]   2008026567

Chelsea House books are available at special discounts when purchased in bulk quantities for businesses, associations, institutions, or sales promotions. Please call our Special Sales Department in New York at (212) 967-8800 or (800) 322-8755.

You can find Chelsea House on the World Wide Web at http://www.chelseahouse.com

Text design by Erik Lindstrom
Cover design by Takeshi Takahashi

Printed in the United States of America

Bang EJB 10 9 8 7 6 5 4 3 2 1

This book is printed on acid-free paper.

All links and Web addresses were checked and verified to be correct at the time of publication. Because of the dynamic nature of the Web, some addresses and links may have changed since publication and may no longer be valid.

TABLE OF CONTENTS

Arthur M. Schlesinger, Jr.

On Leadership

Leadership, it may be said, is really what makes the world go round. Love no doubt smoothes the passage; but love is a private transaction between consenting adults. Leadership is a public transaction with history. The idea of leadership affirms the capacity of individuals to move, inspire, and mobilize masses of people so that they act together in pursuit of an end. Sometimes leadership serves good purposes, sometimes bad; but whether the end is benign or evil, great leaders are those men and women who leave their personal stamp on history.

Now, the very concept of leadership implies the proposition that individuals can make a difference. This proposition has never been universally accepted. From classical times to the present day, eminent thinkers have regarded individuals as no more than the agents and pawns of larger forces, whether the gods and goddesses of the ancient world or, in the modern era, race, class, nation, the dialectic, the will of the people, the spirit of the times, history itself. Against such forces, the individual dwindles into insignificance.

So contends the thesis of historical determinism. Tolstoy's great novel *War and Peace* offers a famous statement of the case. Why, Tolstoy asked, did millions of men in the Napoleonic Wars, denying their human feelings and their common sense, move back and forth across Europe slaughtering their fellows? "The war," Tolstoy answered, "was bound to happen simply because it was bound to happen." All prior history determined it. As for leaders, they, Tolstoy said, "are but the labels that serve to give a name to an end and, like labels, they have the least possible connection with the event." The greater the leader, "the more conspicuous the inevitability and the predestination of every act he commits." The leader, said Tolstoy, is "the slave of history."

Determinism takes many forms. Marxism is the determinism of class. Nazism the determinism of race. But the idea of men and women as the slaves of history runs athwart the deepest human instincts. Rigid determinism abolishes the idea of human freedom—the assumption of free choice that underlies every move we make, every word we speak, every thought we think. It abolishes the idea of human responsibility, since it is manifestly unfair to reward or punish people for actions that are by definition beyond their control. No one can live consistently by any deterministic creed. The Marxist states prove this themselves by their extreme susceptibility to the cult of leadership.

More than that, history refutes the idea that individuals make no difference. In December 1931, a British politician crossing Fifth Avenue in New York City between 76th and 77th streets around 10:30 P.M. looked in the wrong direction and was knocked down by an automobile—a moment, he later recalled, of a man aghast, a world aglare: "I do not understand why I was not broken like an eggshell or squashed like a gooseberry." Fourteen months later an American politician, sitting in an open car in Miami, Florida, was fired on by an assassin; the man beside him was hit. Those who believe that individuals make no difference to history might well ponder whether the next two decades would have been the same had Mario Constasino's car killed Winston Churchill in 1931 and Giuseppe Zangara's bullet killed Franklin Roosevelt in 1933. Suppose, in addition, that Lenin had died of typhus in Siberia in 1895 and that Hitler had been killed on the western front in 1916. What would the twentieth century have looked like now?

For better or for worse, individuals do make a difference. "The notion that a people can run itself and its affairs anonymously," wrote the philosopher William James, "is now well known to be the silliest of absurdities. Mankind does nothing save through initiatives on the part of inventors, great or small, and imitation by the rest of us—these are the sole factors in human progress. Individuals of genius show the way, and set the patterns, which common people then adopt and follow."

Leadership, James suggests, means leadership in thought as well as in action. In the long run, leaders in thought may well make the greater difference to the world. "The ideas of economists and political philosophers, both when they are right and when they are wrong," wrote John Maynard Keynes, "are more powerful than is commonly understood. Indeed the world is ruled by little else. Practical men, who believe themselves to be quite exempt from any intellectual influences, are usually the slaves of some defunct economist . . . . The power of vested interests is vastly exaggerated compared with the gradual encroachment of ideas."

But, as Woodrow Wilson once said, "Those only are leaders of men, in the general eye, who lead in action . . . . It is at their hands that new thought gets its translation into the crude language of deeds." Leaders in thought often invent in solitude and obscurity, leaving to later generations the tasks of imitation. Leaders in action—the leaders portrayed in this series—have to be effective in their own time.

And they cannot be effective by themselves. They must act in response to the rhythms of their age. Their genius must be adapted, in a phrase from William James, "to the receptivities of the moment." Leaders are useless without followers. "There goes the mob," said the French politician, hearing a clamor in the streets. "I am their leader. I must follow them." Great leaders turn the inchoate emotions of the mob to purposes of their own. They seize on the opportunities of their time, the hopes, fears, frustrations, crises, potentialities. They succeed when events have prepared the way for them, when the community is awaiting to be aroused, when they can provide the clarifying and organizing ideas. Leadership completes the circuit between the individual and the mass and thereby alters history.

It may alter history for better or for worse. Leaders have been responsible for the most extravagant follies and most monstrous crimes that have beset suffering humanity. They have also been vital in such gains as humanity has made in individual freedom, religious and racial tolerance, social justice, and respect for human rights.

There is no sure way to tell in advance who is going to lead for good and who for evil. But a glance at the gallery of men and women in MODERN WORLD LEADERS suggests some useful tests.

One test is this: Do leaders lead by force or by persuasion? By command or by consent? Through most of history leadership was exercised by the divine right of authority. The duty of followers was to defer and to obey. "Theirs not to reason why/Theirs but to do and die." On occasion, as with the so-called enlightened despots of the eighteenth century in Europe, absolutist leadership was animated by humane purposes. More often, absolutism nourished the passion for domination, land, gold, and conquest and resulted in tyranny.

The great revolution of modern times has been the revolution of equality. "Perhaps no form of government," wrote the British historian James Bryce in his study of the United States, *The American Commonwealth*, "needs great leaders so much as democracy." The idea that all people should be equal in their legal condition has undermined the old structure of authority, hierarchy, and deference. The revolution of equality has had two contrary effects on the nature of leadership. For equality, as Alexis de Tocqueville pointed out in his great study *Democracy in America*, might mean equality in servitude as well as equality in freedom.

"I know of only two methods of establishing equality in the political world," Tocqueville wrote. "Rights must be given to every citizen, or none at all to anyone ... save one, who is the master of all." There was no middle ground "between the sovereignty of all and the absolute power of one man." In his astonishing prediction of twentieth-century totalitarian dictatorship, Tocqueville explained how the revolution of equality could lead to the *Führerprinzip* and more terrible absolutism than the world had ever known.

But when rights are given to every citizen and the sovereignty of all is established, the problem of leadership takes a new form, becomes more exacting than ever before. It is easy to issue commands and enforce them by the rope and the stake, the concentration camp and the *gulag*. It is much harder to use argument and achievement to overcome opposition and win consent. The Founding Fathers of the United States understood the difficulty. They believed that history had given them the opportunity to decide, as Alexander Hamilton wrote in the first Federalist Paper, whether men are indeed capable of basing government on "reflection and choice, or whether they are forever destined to depend … on accident and force."

Government by reflection and choice called for a new style of leadership and a new quality of followership. It required leaders to be responsive to popular concerns, and it required followers to be active and informed participants in the process. Democracy does not eliminate emotion from politics; sometimes it fosters demagoguery; but it is confident that, as the greatest of democratic leaders put it, you cannot fool all of the people all of the time. It measures leadership by results and retires those who overreach or falter or fail.

It is true that in the long run despots are measured by results too. But they can postpone the day of judgment, sometimes indefinitely, and in the meantime they can do infinite harm. It is also true that democracy is no guarantee of virtue and intelligence in government, for the voice of the people is not necessarily the voice of God. But democracy, by assuring the right of opposition, offers built-in resistance to the evils inherent in absolutism. As the theologian Reinhold Niebuhr summed it up, "Man's capacity for justice makes democracy possible, but man's inclination to justice makes democracy necessary."

A second test for leadership is the end for which power is sought. When leaders have as their goal the supremacy of a master race or the promotion of totalitarian revolution or the acquisition and exploitation of colonies or the protection of greed and privilege or the preservation of personal power, it is likely that their leadership will do little to advance the cause of humanity. When their goal is the abolition of slavery, the liberation of women, the enlargement of opportunity for the poor and powerless, the extension of equal rights to racial minorities, the defense of the freedoms of expression and opposition, it is likely that their leadership will increase the sum of human liberty and welfare.

Leaders have done great harm to the world. They have also conferred great benefits. You will find both sorts in this series. Even "good" leaders must be regarded with a certain wariness. Leaders are not demigods; they put on their trousers one leg after another just like ordinary mortals. No leader is infallible, and every leader needs to be reminded of this at regular intervals. Irreverence irritates leaders but is their salvation. Unquestioning submission corrupts leaders and demeans followers. Making a cult of a leader is always a mistake. Fortunately hero worship generates its own antidote. "Every hero," said Emerson, "becomes a bore at last."

The single benefit the great leaders confer is to embolden the rest of us to live according to our own best selves, to be active, insistent, and resolute in affirming our own sense of things. For great leaders attest to the reality of human freedom against the supposed inevitabilities of history. And they attest to the wisdom and power that may lie within the most unlikely of us, which is why Abraham Lincoln remains the supreme example of great leadership. A great leader, said Emerson, exhibits new possibilities to all humanity. "We feed on genius . . . . Great men exist that there may be greater men."

Great leaders, in short, justify themselves by emancipating and empowering their followers. So humanity struggles to master its destiny, remembering with Alexis de Tocqueville: "It is true that around every man a fatal circle is traced beyond which he cannot pass; but within the wide verge of that circle he is powerful and free; as it is with man, so with communities." ●

1

The Risk Taker

THERE ARE MOMENTS IN THE LIFE OF A POLITICIAN OR ANY PUBLIC FIGURE that seem to sum up who that person is. That moment, good or bad, comes to symbolize to the public that person both as a public figure and as an individual.

For many Americans, former New York City mayor Rudolph Giuliani is indelibly remembered for the leadership that he displayed immediately following the events of 9/11. In other examples, Martin Luther King Jr. is embodied by his famous "I have a dream" speech. Jacqueline Kennedy Onassis will always be the elegant figure swathed in black at her husband's funeral.

The same process takes place in other nations as well. In France, for example, Nicolas Sarkozy, the nation's president, is for many best understood, best represented by one moment in 1993.

"My back was soaked, I could hear the sweat trickling down it: It was fear, fear of doing a bad job."

—Nicolas Sarkozy

Philippe Labro, a novelist and talk-show host, recalled the events in the article "The Human Bomb," published in the August 27, 2007, issue of the *New Yorker*.

It was in 1993, when Sarkozy was mayor of [Paris suburb] Neuilly. A psychotic took over a nursery school. He strapped explosives to his body, and he held the children hostage. He called himself H.B., the human bomb. He had an incoherent set of demands—a true lunatic—and the police surrounded the place. Sarkozy went into the school, completely alone, and began to talk to the human bomb. He engaged him in conversation: what did he want, what were his problems, could he solve them? But first he had to let the children go. Well, half an hour later, out comes Nicolas with children in his arms and all around him. Later, of course, the police went in and shot the human bomb dead.

This was the first time that many people in France had even heard of Nicolas Sarkozy. That was the moment he was introduced to the French people. Two things were apparent. Courage? Yes. But also an almost crazy appetite for living on the edge that is completely outside the normal experience of French politicians. He *likes* risks, enjoys risks, revels in risks.

This is not to say the need or ability to perform such acts of courage comes easily, or that Nicolas Sarkozy does not recognize the risks he takes and is never afraid. After the "human bomb" incident, he said afterward, as quoted in the *New York*

During his term as mayor of Neuilly-sur-Seine, a suburb of Paris, Nicolas Sarkozy put himself in the line of fire and directly negotiated with a mad gunman who had taken over a nursery school. Sarkozy's ability to bargain successfully with the hostage taker made him a national hero. *Above*, parents, firefighters, and police officers wait outside the nursery school in Neuilly-sur-Seine during the tense standoff.

Sun, "My back was soaked, I could hear the sweat trickling down it: It was fear, fear of doing a bad job." For Sarkozy, however, conquering his fear and taking a risk paid off: both for himself and the young hostages.

Fourteen years later, Nicolas Sarkozy was one of the two major candidates for the presidency of France. Although leading his rival Ségolène Royal in the polls, he was the target of attack videos shown on the Internet. These videos envisioned life in France under Sarkozy's rule—a vision of France, as Doreen Carvajal described it in the *International Herald Tribune*, as "riot police, burning cars, and suburbs engulfed in violence."

Faced with these attack ads, Sarkozy's election team responded with a video of its own. The five-minute video, entitled "Human Bomb," utilized news footage of Sarkozy negotiating with the human bomb and personally bringing the children to safety. Accompanied by music from the movie *Gladiator*, the video was seen by more than 450,000 viewers and gave a compelling and memorable human and emotional picture of Sarkozy. It gave an image of Sarkozy as a man of action, a risk taker, a man who achieved results.

"We know there was a huge impact on people seeing the 'Human Bomb,'" said campaign consultant Arnaud Dassier in the *International Herald Tribune*, who organized the campaign's Internet activities. (The ad is posted at www.dailymotion.com/video/x1tber_sarkozy_human-bomb.)

Sarkozy's risk paid off. His act of courage in 1993 was a decisive factor in his winning the presidency of France in 2007. Other political risks of his have failed to pay off. In 1995, to the surprise of many, Sarkozy turned his back on his long-time political mentor Jacques Chirac, and endorsed Chirac's opponent, Édouard Balladur, for the office of president of France.

It was a bold and risky political gamble. When Chirac won the presidency, Sarkozy lost his position as minister for the budget and found himself stranded well outside the circles of power. It would take several years for him to rebuild his political capital, only to see it slip once again following the disastrous 1999 European Parliament elections.

AN UNLIKELY TALE

Still, he made yet another political comeback, climbing ever closer to the top of the political pyramid until finally, on

May 16, 2007, Nicolas Sarkozy became the president of France. It was an unlikely climax to a remarkable political career. Indeed, as Tim King pointed out in a portrait of Sarkozy published in the July 2004 issue of *Prospect* magazine, "If Sarkozy were a character in a work of fiction, he would strain credibility." In other words, his life has been a fantastic, incredible journey.

Consider the following. Sarkozy's father, a Hungarian aristocrat stripped of his titles and wealth, joined the French foreign legion in order to escape Stalin. He eventually ended up in Paris, where he married a law student of Greek and Jewish heritage. Shortly after the birth of the couple's third child, he abandoned his family, leaving young Nicolas to his own devices, which largely consisted of entertaining himself watching television alone at home.

Consider this as well. Nicolas Sarkozy is a right-wing politician in a left-leaning country. He is a child of immigrants who has made his reputation being tough on immigration.

He has made it a habit to latch on to older political figures, only to ultimately betray them in order to climb up the next rung of the political ladder. A child of a broken home, he divorced his first wife and married a woman who was also divorced. During the course of his second marriage, both he and his wife had public extramarital affairs. Not long after divorcing his second wife, his whirlwind courtship and marriage to singer and former fashion model Carla Bruni captivated the country and the entire world. By most standards, Nicolas Sarkozy has been a most untraditional politician.

It is important to realize that even in France, Nicolas Sarkozy is far from being universally loved. The first French president in decades to label himself as being politically on the "right," he is deeply disliked and distrusted by many on the left of the French political spectrum. To them, Sarkozy is a political demagogue, a politician who appeals to people's darkest fears and prejudices in order to gain power. He has been called

A tireless workaholic, Nicolas Sarkozy *(above)* is often described as hyper-active, ambitious, and unafraid. His vision for France involves controversial changes for its people, including pension and union reform and improved relations with the United States.

"[SARKOZY] DOESN'T WANT YOU TO LIKE HIM. HE WANTS YOU TO HELP HIM GET THINGS DONE."

—Jean-Michel Goudard

arrogant and brutal, and has been accused of being willing to trade away civil liberties for political gains. He is seen by the traditional French ruling class as an outsider, as someone who did not come from the "right family," or go to the "right schools." He is a polarizing figure, among the most liked and disliked political figures in France today.

To Nicolas Sarkozy, however, taking political risks and striving to bring about change means accepting the risk of becoming unpopular. As Sarkozy's communications director, Jean-Michel Goudard, told Jan Kramer in the April 23, 2007, issue of the *New Yorker*, "He is unafraid. He doesn't want you to like him. He wants you to help him get things done."

It is all a part of politics, and for Sarkozy, worth the risk. Because for Sarkozy, a career in politics has always been his life's interest, his life's dream. As he said in his book, *Testimony*,

> . . . it's politics that has attracted all my interest and desire at least since I was fifteen years old. I did not choose to go into politics. I never said to myself, "I would like to go into politics." It just happened—naturally and irresistibly. That's why I've never really tried to explain it . . . It was something deep inside me, and it would have been unnatural for me not to follow it. This is no doubt why—notwithstanding all the obstacles I've had to overcome, all the failures I've had to endure, all the tests I've had to pass—this passion kept me going.

Anita Hausser, who wrote a biography of Sarkozy, says about him that "he's hyperactive, he's ambitious, he's a heavy worker, a workaholic, he never rests." Ambition is a key element to Sarkozy's personality. Indeed, as Andre Santini, a centrist Parliament member said in the biography *Nicolas Sarkozy Au Fond Des Yeux*, "I have known Nicolas since he was 18. I was already elected in Courbevoie and we would meet with a friend to eat ice-creams at the drugstore of Neuilly. He was already telling us he would be president of the republic one day."

Where did Sarkozy's confidence come from? How did this child of immigrants climb the ranks to become the French president? What are his ideas and policies that make him both respected and feared by the people of France? What is his vision for France? In other words, who exactly is French president Nicolas Sarkozy?

2

A Family of Immigrants

LIKE MANY COUNTRIES AROUND THE WORLD, FRANCE IS BEING REMADE by immigrants. Nicolas Sarkozy himself is a child of such immigrants.

His father was named Pal Sarkozy de Nagy-Bocsa (in Hungarian, Nagobocasi Sarkozy Pal, and some sources spell it Nagy-Bocasy). Pal Sarkozy was born in 1928 in Budapest, Hungary, into a family belonging to the lower ranks of the nobility. As wealthy nobles, both Pal's father and grandfather held elective offices in the town of Szolnok. Although the Sarkozy de Nagy-Bocsa family was Protestant, Pal Sarkozy's mother, Katalin Toth de Csaford, grandmother of Nicolas Sarkozy, was a descendant of a Catholic aristocratic family.

In the year 1944, World War II was entering its final stages. Hungary, a one-time ally of Nazi Germany, after suffering major losses at the river Don, attempted to negotiate terms of surrender with the allies. Germany was unwilling to accept the loss of Hungary and sent its own troops into Hungary to occupy the nation and install a pro-German government. With that, Russian troops invaded Hungary, and the Sarkozy family fled to Germany to escape the Red Army.

They returned to Hungary in 1945, but found that all their possessions and land had been seized by the government as the country, occupied by the Red Army, fell under the influence of Communist Russia. Pal Sarkozy's father and grandfather died shortly thereafter, leaving Pal and his mother to survive on their own.

Pal's mother was terrified that her son would be drafted into the Hungarian People's Army, or even worse, sent to prison in Siberia as an "enemy of the people" for his aristocratic origins. She urged Pal Sarkozy, then only 17 years old, to flee to Paris, promising him that she would follow him as soon as she was able.

Pal managed to escape into Austria and then on to Germany, while his mother, Katalin, informed Hungarian authorities that her son had drowned in Lake Balaton. Pal Sarkozy eventually arrived in Baden Baden, the headquarters of the French army in Germany and near the French border. Broke and homeless, it was there that Pal would meet a recruiter from the French foreign legion.

THE FRENCH FOREIGN LEGION

Established in 1831 by King Louis Philippe of France, the French foreign legion is a unique elect unit within the French army created for foreign volunteers. The legion was primarily used to protect and to help expand the French colonial empire during the nineteenth century, but it also fought in all of France's wars including both World Wars.

Many people have a romantic image of the legion as a refuge where criminals and other people on the run could join to start a new life with a new identity. While that is partially true, historically, the ranks of the legion have been filled with enlistees from countries that were undergoing some sort of crisis, with many recruits being foreigners who found themselves in France and out of work, men just like Pal Sarkozy.

Training for the legion is known to be extremely difficult, both physically and psychologically, with the goal of uniting a disparate group of men of different backgrounds and nationalities. After three years in the legion, a legionnaire of foreign nationality can ask for and receive French citizenship.

For Pal, joining the legion seemed an obvious way to help him start a new life. He signed up for five years and was immediately sent for training to Sidi Bel Abbes, in French Algeria, where the French foreign legion's headquarters was located. (Algeria, a country located in North Africa, was an important part of France from the time that France invaded in 1830 until Algeria finally achieved independence in 1962).

At the end of his training, Pal Sarkozy was scheduled to complete his service in Indochina, where the French were fighting an ultimately losing battle against the Viet Minh, who were struggling for Vietnamese independence. Fortunately for Pal, the doctor who checked him before his departure was also Hungarian. He sympathized with his countryman and gave him a medical discharge, possibly saving him from death at the hands of the Viet Minh.

Now freed from his obligations to the legion, Pal Sarkozy returned to civilian life in 1948, settling in Marseille, and changing the spelling of his name from the Hungarian "Pal" to the French Paul Sarkozy de Nagy-Bocsa. One year later, in 1949, he met Andree Mallah, Nicolas Sarkozy's mother.

FLEEING TO SAFETY

Andree Mallah was a law student when she met Pal Sarkozy. She was the daughter of Benedict Mallah, a wealthy and noted urologist and STD (sexually transmitted disease) specialist with a well-established reputation among the mainly bourgeois (middle-class) residents of Paris's 17th arrondissement. (The

After the Soviet invasion of Hungary near the end of World War II, Nicolas Sarkozy's father was urged by his mother to leave their native country. He eventually reached France and joined the French foreign legion. *Above,* Soviet soldiers attack an enemy strong point in Hungary during World War II.

city of Paris is divided into 20 separate arrondissements, or municipal boroughs, each with its own individual character.)

Benedict Mallah, originally called Aron Mallah and nicknamed Benkio, was born in 1890 in the Sephardic Jewish community of Salonika (Thessaloníki), located in Greece. (A Sephardic Jew is one whose origins are in the Iberian Peninsula—Spain or Portugal. The majority of Jews are Ashkenazi, who originated in Eastern Europe.)

According to research done by Jewish genealogical societies, the Mallah family of Salonika came there from Spain, which they had fled in 1492 when the Catholic monarchs King

Although he was christened and raised a Catholic, Nicolas Sarkozy continues to identify with his Jewish ancestry. One of the promises he made during his campaign for the French presidency was to end intolerance, including racism. *Above*, Sarkozy visits the Holocaust museum in Budapest, Hungary, the native country of his father.

Ferdinand and Queen Isabella expelled all Jews from the country. (This is the same King Ferdinand and Queen Isabella who sponsored Christopher Columbus's voyage to the New World.) After first settling in Provence, in southern France, the family moved to Salonika a century later.

Greece's second largest city and the capital of Macedonia, Salonika has been a cultural center for Christians, Muslims and Jews for centuries. While the first-recorded Jews in the city arrived from Alexandria, Egypt, Jews from Provence, France, and southern Italy also settled in the city, fleeing persecution in their native lands. It was not until the fifteenth century, however, with a large influx of Sephardic Jews (including the Mallah family), that Salonika achieved fame as a "Jewish" city and was given the unofficial name *La Madre de Israel* ("the mother of Israel").

Interestingly, even though the city was under the control of the Ottoman (Turkish) Empire, and so nominally Muslim, the Jewish immigrants were welcomed into the life of the city. For four centuries, Sephardic Jews, Muslims, and Greek Orthodox Christians lived peacefully together and remained the principal groups in the city. In fact, for 200 years Salonika was the largest Jewish city in the world; of its 130,000 inhabitants at the start of the twentieth century, over 60,000 were Sephardic Jews.

The Mallah family did extraordinarily well in Salonika, becoming prominent Zionist leaders and playing vital roles in the city's political, economic, social, and cultural life. Among the members of the family were famous jewelers, a Rabbi who edited a prominent Zionist newspaper, a senator in the Greek senate, and noted philanthropists. Aron left Salonika in 1904 at the young age of 14, accompanied by his mother, to attend the prestigious Lycee Lakanal boarding school, located just outside of Paris. They were joined by many other members of the family in 1917, after a fire destroyed a major part of the old Jewish quarter of Salonika and heavily damaged the family estate.

Aron studied medicine after receiving his baccalaureate and decided to remain in France and become a French citizen. Not only did he become a citizen, he converted to Catholicism and changed his name to Benedict so that he could marry a French Christian woman named Adele Bouvier. The couple had two daughters, Susanne and Andree. (It is said, though, that Benedict never again entered a church after his wedding day, but then he never went back to synagogue, either. This enabled him to fit into and prosper in France's highly secularized society.)

Although the family was fully integrated into French society, when Germany invaded and occupied France during World War II, Benedict and his family were forced to escape from Paris and find refuge in a small farm in Marcillac la Croisille in the Corrèze region of western France. For despite the fact that Benedict had become a Catholic, the Nazis still considered him to be Jewish by blood. Because of this, he and his family risked being arrested and handed over to the Germans if they remained in Paris.

Benedict, his wife, and their two daughters all survived the war. Others in his family were not so fortunate. During the Holocaust, many of the Mallahs who had remained in Salonika or had moved to France and *not* gone into hiding were deported to concentration camps. Fifty-seven members of the Mallah family were brutally murdered by the Nazis, simply because they were Jewish.

(In July of 2006, while visiting Greece, Nicolas Sarkozy was honored at the French embassy in Athens by the Jewish community of Salonika. A plaque was unveiled that read, "In memory of Nicolas Sarkozy's visit to Greece from the Thessaloníki Jewish Community, the town of your ancestors, mother and city of Israel and Jerusalem of the Balkans." Along with the plaque, Sarkozy was presented with an album of his family tree, reaching back to his great-great-grandfather along with pictures of his ancestors. Deeply and obviously moved, Sarkozy thanked the community and said, "My roots are here.")

Indeed, it is interesting to note that even though Nicolas Sarkozy is Catholic, he still feels a strong and deep connection to his Jewish roots and to the nation of Israel. In a 2004 interview, published in the book *La Règublique, les religions, l'espérance* (the republic, religion, and hope), Sarkozy said,

> Should I remind you the visceral attachment of every Jew to Israel, as a second mother homeland? There is nothing out-rageous about it. Every Jew carries within him a fear passed down through generations, and he knows that if one day he will not feel safe in his country, there will always be a place that would welcome him.

Paul Sarkozy, who Nicholas Simon described in his article "The Jewish Vote and the French Election," as "a tall, seduc-tive man who dabbled in art, advertising and bankruptcy," met Andree Mallah in Paris in 1949. At that time, Andree was attending law school, a somewhat bold and unorthodox choice of study for a French woman of that time. One year later, in 1950, the couple had married and settled in the 17th arrondisse-ment in Paris. Andree left school and started a family.

The couple had three sons: Guillaume, born in 1951, is an entrepreneur in the textile industry; Nicolas, born Nicolas Paul Stephane Sarkozy de Nagy-Bocsa on January 28, 1955; and François born in 1957, manager of a health-care consultancy company. Paul and Andree's marriage, though, would not last. One day in 1959, Paul Sarkozy walked out the door, leaving behind his wife and their three children. Nicolas was just four years old, and his life would never be the same.

3

Early Life and Education

IT IS IMPORTANT TO REMEMBER THAT IN 1960, AROUND THE TIME THAT Paul Sarkozy abandoned his family, family life was much more stable than it is today and divorce much less common. In 1960, for example, only a little more than one in ten marriages ended in divorce. Today it is one in three. To be a child of divorce, living with a single mother, was much rarer then than it is today.

Andree was left on her own. Her former husband, even though he had become wealthy from the founding of his own advertising agency, refused to give his family any financial support, forcing Andree to take legal action. Paul Sarkozy, a man who owned, according to the *Daily Telegraph*, several houses and two yachts, and collected paintings by Picasso and Matisse, won the case after convincing the judge he owned almost nothing. He was driven away from court in a limousine.

As young as he was, the outcome of his parent's divorce taught Nicolas a lesson. As quoted by Henry Samuel in the

Daily Telegraph, "The fear of tomorrow, unless it paralyzes you, pushes you to work more than others. To get out of that fear, you need to sweep away the obstacles and keep at it."

THE ABSENCE OF A FATHER

After divorcing Nicolas's mother, Paul Sarkozy married two more times and had two more children. Occupied with business concerns and his new family, Paul had little interest in spending time with his old family. Nicolas felt abandoned by his father, which, along with feelings of insecurity caused by chubbiness, lack of physical stature and his family's lack of money (at least compared to their neighbors), led to feelings of humiliation. Still, as for many others, an unhappy childhood can be the impetus, the driving force, to do what is necessary to change one's life. As Sarkozy himself said, quoted in Catherine Ney's biography, "What made me who I am now is the sum of all the humiliations suffered during childhood."

He elaborated on this further in his interview with Charlie Rose on January 31, 2007, saying,

> Perhaps if I had had a normal family, then I wouldn't have the energy I have now . . . I've always had to fight throughout my life. Nothing has ever been easy. Nothing has ever come easily to me. Nobody has ever opened any doors to me. I've had to push the doors open. And I got used to that. Life is a struggle. I'm living on my feet, not on my back.

Though in many ways Nicolas Sarkozy's childhood was a struggle, in other ways he was lucky. Even though his real father had abandoned him and his family, he did have someone else to fall back on, someone who would quickly become the prominent male figure in his life.

Because of Paul's refusal to provide his family with financial support, Andree was forced to move back home to live with her father while resuming her study of the law. Nicolas's grandfather, Benedict, who had been a widower for three years, was delighted to have his daughter and three grandsons live with him. He became the main male influence in Nicolas Sarkozy's life, becoming almost like a father to him. In Ney's semi-authorized biography, Sarkozy discusses in detail just how much he admired his grandfather. He described the many happy hours he spent listening to him tell stories of what life was like living under Nazi occupation, heroic stories of the French resistance, and most especially, tales of his personal hero, General Charles de Gaulle, and stories of liberation from Nazi rule.

CHARLES DE GAULLE AND LOVE OF COUNTRY

To many French citizens, Charles de Gaulle (November 22, 1890–November 9, 1970) represented the best of French strength and patriotism. The leader of the Free French government-in-exile during Nazi occupation, de Gaulle became the head of the French provisional government from 1946 to 1949 and ultimately served as France's first president of the Fifth Republic from 1958 to 1969. (The Fifth Republic, 1958–present, represents France's fifth attempt at a republican form of government since the French Revolution of 1789 that overthrew the monarchy. Indeed, as novelist Gore Vidal once pointed out, since then, France's forms of government have included one directory, one consulate, two empires, three restorations of the monarchy, and five republics.)

General de Gaulle's political ideology became known as Gaullism (a reference to both Charles de Gaulle and the word "Gaul" the Roman name for the region that includes modern-day France), and it has been a major influence on all subsequent French politics. Holding itself above parties and left-right distinctions, it is characterized by a belief in the historical destiny of a strong, independent France. Generally considered to be a social-conservative moment, a direct line can be traced from de Gaulle's own political party, the Union of Democrats for

Time spent with his grandfather, Benedict, greatly influenced Sarkozy's political views. Benedict's nationalism and support of Gaullism, a political ideology developed by French general Charles de Gaulle, fostered a deep love for France, its people and its culture in Sarkozy. *Above*, de Gaulle (in uniform) leads a victory parade in Paris after the liberation of France from German forces in World War II.

the Republic to today's Union for a Popular Movement, led by Nicolas Sarkozy. A large part of Sarkozy's political thought and beliefs comes from his grandfather, Benedict.

As Sarkozy describes in his book, *Testimony*, even at an early age, he had an idea of France and Gaullism's role in the country,

IT WAS HIS GRANDFATHER WHO SHOWED YOUNG NICOLAS THAT THE WORLD WAS, INDEED, AN EXTRAORDINARY PLACE.

. . . we loved France. We didn't take it for granted. Throughout my childhood, perched on the shoulders of my grandfather, I was always fascinated and moved by the annual Armistice Day and Bastille Day parades. I never got tired of watching them, and it would never have occurred to me to criticize France.

If "admiration is the source of every vocation," as the writer Michel Tournier has said, I must also mention General Charles de Gaulle, and Gaullism in particular. . . . Gaullism overcame all political and social divisions and brought millions of French people of different backgrounds and social classes together behind a "certain idea of France" and a desire to modernize and transform France. I was fascinated by this ability to break habits and traditions in leading an entire country to excellence.

This desire to bring France together, to transform it to achieve greatness, learned from his grandfather, is what drove Nicolas Sarkozy into politics.

Benedict Mallah influenced his grandson in other ways as well. The Sephardic Jew who had converted to Catholicism raised Nicolas and his brothers in the Catholic faith of the household. Sarkozy, like his brothers, is a baptized and professed Catholic. Indeed, Sarkozy is on record as saying that one of his role models is the late Pope John Paul II.

Most of all, however, it was his grandfather who showed young Nicolas, disheartened and confused by the absence of his father, that the world was, indeed, an extraordinary place. He discussed this in an interview with Charlie Rose,

I was brought up by my grandfather. Every day, he would say to me, you're going to be living in a tremendous world, an extraordinary world. And when we went off on an outing, if I didn't have school, my grandfather took me by my hand and we went off to the metro station [subway] nearby. We got into the metro and we went right through to the end of the line, without saying a word to each other. And we went into the first café. He had a coffee and I had an orange juice. And he then said one thing to me. He said, "You're going to live in an extraordinary world." Nowadays, who tells their children the world is extraordinary? The future has become a threat.

Financially unable to send her children to the private schools that educated the children who would grow up to become France's political elite, Nicolas Sarkozy was enrolled in the Lycée Chaptal, a state-funded middle and high school in the 8th arrondissement. There, he failed his *sixieme* (the equivalent to sixth grade in the United States) exams. By this time, Andree had graduated from law school and gotten a job, and she was able to send Nicolas and his brothers to the Cours Saint-Louis de Monceau, a private Catholic school in the 17th arrondissement.

Nicolas had a reputation as being a mediocre student. His father, on one of the rare times he spent time with Nicolas, predicted a lackluster future for him, saying "With the name you carry and the results you obtain, you will never succeed in France." What he was trying to warn Nicolas about was that *because* he was the child of immigrants, he would have to have outstanding grades and work that much harder to have any chance of succeeding in French society. Such comments only drove Nicolas farther away from his father, while at the same time making him more determined than ever to prove him wrong.

1968

The year 1968 was one of political turmoil and student unrest throughout the world. In the United States, students throughout the country protested against the Vietnam War, and in just one instance, occupied and forced the closure of Columbia University. In Mexico, on October 2, 1968, a demonstration ended in the death of an estimated 200–300 unarmed protestors in what has become known as the Tlatelolco Massacre. Students protested, as well, in Germany, Belgium, and throughout Eastern Europe. France, too, became a center of student protests, in the series of events that have come to be known as May '68.

It began as a series of student strikes following the arrest of more than 100 protesting students at Nanterre University on March 22. By May 2, protests caused the administration to shut down the University of Paris at Nanterre, which led to student protests and police action at the University of the Sorbonne in Paris the next day. On May 6, the national student union, the UNEF (still the largest student union in France today), along with the union of university teachers, called for a march to protest against the police invasion of the Sorbonne. More than 20,000 students, teachers, and supporters marched toward the Sorbonne, still sealed off by the police. The police charged at the marchers, and the crowd dispersed, building barricades, while others threw paving stones. The police responded with tear gas, charging the crowd again. Hundreds more students were arrested.

High school students started to go on strike in support of the students at the Sorbonne and Nanterre, joining the rapidly growing crowd of students, teachers, and young workers demanding that the arrested protestors be released and the schools be reopened. On May 10, another huge crowd gathered in protest. When the riot police blocked the protestors from crossing the Seine River, the crowd again threw up barricades, and once again the police attacked, producing hundreds of arrests and injuries.

The government's heavy-handed response to the protestors created a wave of sympathy for the students. The French Communist Party supported the students, and the major left union federations called a one-day general strike and demonstration for May 13. More than one million people marched through Paris on that day, while the police stayed out of sight. In response to the growing number of protestors, Prime Minister Georges Pompidou personally announced the release of the prisoners and the reopening of the Sorbonne. It was too late, though, to stop the protests.

When the Sorbonne reopened, it was quickly occupied by the students and declared an autonomous "people's university." Approximately 401 popular "action committees" were set up in Paris and elsewhere. In the following days, workers began occupying factories. By May 16, workers had taken control of and occupied roughly 50 factories. By May 17, 200,000 workers were on strike. That figure exploded to two million workers on strike the following day, and then to ten million, nearly two-thirds of the French workforce, on strike the following week.

But what was it that the strikers wanted? While the unions tried to channel the strikes into a struggle for higher wages and other economic demands, the workers pushed for a broader, more political agenda. They demanded the ouster of the government and of President Charles de Gaulle, as well as worker control of the factories themselves.

The trade-union leadership negotiated large increases in both the minimum wage and wages for other workers, but the workers occupying the factories still refused to return to work. On May 30, 300,000–400,000 protestors marched through the streets of Paris, chanting, "Adieu, de Gaulle!" ("Good-bye, de Gaulle!") Though the government seemed close to collapse at one point (de Gaulle was even forced to take temporary refuge at an air-force base in Germany), the crisis soon broke.

After ensuring that he had sufficient support from the military to back him up, de Gaulle went on the radio (the national

In 1968, a small student protest over dormitory rules at a local school unexpectedly escalated into a national strike, stalling work and production in France for several days. It is reported that Nicolas Sarkozy, 13 years old at the time, wished to participate in the counter-demonstrations but was denied permission by his mother due to his age. *Above* demonstrators fight the police in 1968.

television service was on strike) to announce that he was dissolving the National Assembly, with elections to follow on June 23. He ordered workers to return to work and threatened to declare a state of emergency if they did not.

From that point on, the revolutionary feeling of the students and workers began to fade. Workers gradually returned to work, and the national student union called off street demonstrations. The police retook the Sorbonne on June 16, and, somewhat surprisingly, given the strength of the demonstrations, the Gaullist party emerged stronger after the June elections than it had been before the crisis. Obviously, the distinct possibility of revolution, or even civil war, caused the nation to rally around de Gaulle.

Although the Gaullist tradition held strong after the crisis, the era of Charles de Gaulle had come to an end. After losing a referendum to reform the French senate, a vote that was seen as a yes-or-no vote on de Gaulle himself, he resigned as president of France on April 28, 1969. Just a little more than a year later, on November 9, 1970, de Gaulle was dead. The events of May 1968 brought about tremendous change in French society. By standing up against authority, by forcing the government to make major concessions in both education and in wages for the striking workers, the traditionally rigid French society was obliged to relax its rules of conduct. While the Left welcomed the possibility of more change in the future, the traditional right was horrified and appalled by what had taken place that spring of 1968.

Among those alarmed by the student and worker uprising were Nicolas Sarkozy and his family. A traditionalist by nature, and strongly influenced by his grandfather, Nicolas, unlike many of his generation, stood firm in his support of General de Gaulle.

Only 13 years old that fateful spring, as he recalled in his memoir, *Testimony*,

> Because I was too young at the time, my family didn't allow me to participate in the great demonstration supporting General de Gaulle after the massive student and worker protests of May 1968. But, like thousands of other French men and women, I laid a flower under the Arc de Triomphe the day of the great man's funeral in 1970.

Nearly 40 years later, while campaigning to become president of France, Sarkozy harkened back to May 1968. In the same way that United States Republican presidential candidates Ronald Reagan, George H.W. Bush, and George W. Bush ran, in part, against what they saw as the excesses of liberalism in the United States brought about by the student demonstrations of the 1960s, Sarkozy ran against what he saw as the excesses in France caused by the demonstrations of May 1968.

In the last major speech given by Nicolas Sarkozy during his presidential campaign, on April 29, 2007, he explicitly attacked the legacy of the events of May 1968, saying, "In this election, it is a question of whether the heritage of May 1968 should be perpetuated or if it should be liquidated once and for all."

He then seemed to go on to blame the spirit of May 1968 for many, if not most, of France's problems, accusing the Left of "systematically taking the side of thugs, troublemakers and fraudsters against the police." He added that May 1968

> weakened the idea of citizenship by denigrating the law, the state and the nation.... See how the belief in short-term profit and speculation, how the values of financial capitalism grew out of May '68, because there are no more rules, no more norms, no morality, no more respect, no authority.... The heirs of May '68 have imposed the idea that anything goes, that there is no longer any difference between good and evil, no difference between the true and the false, between the beautiful and the ugly ... that the victim counts less than the criminal.

As a Gaullist and spiritual heir of General de Gaulle, Nicolas Sarkozy believes strongly in government, in encouraging people to work, and in pride of country. He believes in the need to break away from May 1968. As he said in a speech two days before the election,

> We have two days left. Two days to liquidate the heritage of May 1968. Two days to renounce passivity. Two days to set free a wave of new energy across the country.... I want to be

able to talk about the nation without being called a national-
ist. I want to be able to talk about protection without being
called a protectionist. I want to be able to talk about authority without being called an authoritarian. . . . I want to be the
spokesman for all the French people.

The result of May 1968, in Sarkozy's view, was a country
afraid of change, a government that was unwilling to exert its
authority, and a nation that had lost pride in itself. Nicolas
Sarkozy was determined to change that.

FINISHING HIS EDUCATION

That would be many years in the future. While the events of
1968 obviously had a significant impact on Sarkozy's political
thought, he was, after all, only 13 when it happened. He still had
a lot of growing up to do and a lot of education to undergo.

After receiving his baccalaureate (known informally in
France as the "bac," it is an academic qualification that French
and international students take at the end of the *lycee*, or high
school), Nicolas Sarkozy enrolled at the Université Paris X
Nanterre. His choice of university is not what one would have
expected.

The University of Paris X, built in the 1960s in the outskirts
of Paris, is an extension of the Sorbonne. It became famous just
after its opening by being at the center of the May '68 student
rebellion. Because of this, the campus was nicknamed *Nanterre,
la folle* ("Mad Nanterre"), or *Nanterre la rouge* ("red Nanterre,"
in reference to communism). To this day, the university remains
a center of the left wing, as opposed to universities such as Paris
II-Assas, traditionally a stronghold of the right.

While there, Sarkozy steered clear of the dominant left-
wing politics of the majority of the students and became
involved in the university's right-wing student union. Although
his political stance was in place, his educational goals were
not. After initially considering journalism and even political

science, he eventually settled, like his mother, on studying law. In 1978, he received his master's degree in private law.

After graduating, Sarkozy tried to continue his education by taking entrance exams to attend the Institut d'Etudes Politiques de Paris (Paris Institute of Political Studies), often referred to as Sciences Po. The school is an elite and highly selective institution. Traditionally, Sciences Po has been one of *the* schools for the French political and diplomatic elite, the school where the ruling class learns how to be the ruling class, where the right people are met and the necessary connections are made to make one's path up the political hill as smooth and trouble free as possible.

Unfortunately for Nicolas Sarkozy, that door slammed shut when he failed his entrance exams, due to, according to biographer Catherine Ney, an insufficient grasp of the English language. (To this day, as he would be the first to admit, his command of English is limited at best. While vacationing in New Hampshire in the summer of 2007, he said, according to April Yee in the *Boston Globe*, that he "was just missing two things: the ability to speak English better, and a boating license. 'My English is so bad,' he said.")

If Sarkozy was going to have a life in politics, it would have to be without the help of a degree earned and connections made at the Institut d'Etudes Politiques de Paris. (He did eventually attend for two years, 1979 to 1981, but left without graduating.) He would still be the outsider, the child of immigrants—the short, chubby kid who did not go to the right schools, who did not come from the right family, who did not have enough money. He would have to begin at the bottom and work his way up, proving himself to a world of political elites that had already rejected him. For Sarkozy that was not a problem. As he once said, "When I'm not invited to dinner, I ring the bell anyway, and it's rare that I'm not asked to stay." If Sarkozy had his way, there would soon be a place for him at the political table.

4

Entering the Arena

SARKOZY'S BASE OF OPERATIONS WOULD BE NEUILLY-SUR-SEINE. THE FAMILY had moved there after leaving grandfather Benedict Mallah's house when Andree had graduated law school and entered the workforce. It would be a perfect place for him to begin his political career.

Neuilly-sur-Seine is a commune bordering on the western limits of the city of Paris, 4.2 miles (6.8 km) from the city center. (A commune is the lowest level of administrative division in the French Republic. French communes are roughly equivalent to incorporated municipalities/cities in the United States. It can be a city of 2 million inhabitants like Paris, a town of 10,000, or just a 10-person village.)

Neuilly-sur-Seine is one of the most densely populated municipalities in Europe, with a population in 2005 of just over 60,000. Neuilly is a wealthy suburb, made up of mostly well-to-do residential neighborhoods; it also hosts the headquarters of

41

R GROSSMANN · P. CAROUS · M DEBRE

Sarkozy soon ascended the ranks of the Union of Democrats for the Republic and began to organize party functions and give speeches on the group's behalf. *Above*, Sarkozy *(third from left)* attends a meeting for the Rally for the Republic political party, as a portrait of the group's founder, Charles de Gaulle *(left)* and his political partner, Georges Pompidou, looms over the members.

many corporations. As such, this would be the electoral base that could respond positively to Sarkozy's conservative message.

BEGINNINGS

Although attired fashionably for the time with long hair and bell-bottomed pants, which would lead one to think that he was a typical young left-winger, Nicolas Sarkozy was deeply involved in conservative-party politics. He had started literally at the bottom, sweeping floors and putting up posters. By the age of 20, however, he was already a party organizer for the Union of Democrats for the Republic, a Gaullist party of France from 1971 to 1976.

(It is important to understand that unlike in the United States, where political parties are long-lasting and stable, French political parties tend to change names and reorganize, even while their basic political positions remain the same. The UDR was the successor to Charles de Gaulle's earlier party, Rally of the French People. It was organized in 1958, at the same time as the founding of the Fifth Republic, as the Union for a New Republic and subsequently merged with the Democratic Union of Labour, a left-Gaullist group in 1962. Five years later, it was joined by some Christian Democrats to form the Union of Democrats for the Fifth Republic, later dropping the "Fifth." Despite the changes, the party survived de Gaulle's death by only six years. It dissolved in 1976, to be succeeded by Jacques Chirac's Rally for the Republic.)

In 1975, the party was still the Union of Democrats for the Republic, and Nicolas Sarkozy was asked to go to the city of Nice to give his first speech at the annual party conference. He was, understandably, so nervous that he could barely breathe. His nerves got even worse when, moments before he was to speak, he was called over by the man who would become his political mentor. He recalled the moment in his memoir, *Testimony*:

> Jacques Chirac was at the time prime minister and leader of the Gaullist movement. He was chairing the conference. Ten minutes before it was my turn to speak, they came to tell me to be ready to go onstage. I was sitting there on a stool that I remember was wobbly—and I was already wondering if this was a bad sign. Then Jacques Chirac called to me: "Are you

Sarkozy? You are speaking for five minutes, and you won't be given a minute more than that, understood?" I went along willingly, without really having understood what had been said to me. My final memory is the moment when, for the first time, I found myself standing behind the podium. I was blinded by the light of the projectors and surprised by the sound of my amplified voice. Curiously, I don't remember anything about what happened later on this day that would determine the orientation of my life. It's as if all that mattered was the starting point.

Indeed, it was the starting point. Although he was given only five minutes to speak, he went on for ten whole minutes, earning a standing ovation when he declared that "being a Gaullist meant being a revolutionary." His speech earned him the attention of Jacques Chirac, the man who would help guide his career by becoming his political mentor, as well as a father figure.

For a young man trying to get ahead in politics, the right mentor can be instrumental in guiding his career. This mentor, someone older, more experienced, and with more connections, can advise him, instruct him, even provide political appointments. In turn, the mentor has a loyal ally, one who will support him, work for him, and help defend him against political adversaries. It can be a perfect relationship for both sides, at least as long as each party can trust the other's loyalty.

Jacques Chirac was an ideal politician to hitch one's star to. After completing his studies at the Institut d'Etudes Politiques de Paris and the Ecole National d'Administration, it was obvious that his was a career destined for greatness. He began his career as a high-level civil servant and soon entered politics, occupying numerous senior positions, including minister of agriculture, prime minister, mayor of Paris, and finally, from 1995 to 2007, president of France. For almost 30 years, Jacques Chirac was the dominant power on the right wing of French politics.

Sarkozy's mentor, Jacques Chirac *(above)*, was a Gaullist with an established career in civil service and politics. While Sarkozy assisted in Chirac's multiple presidential campaigns and was an active conservative, the budding politician did not want to join any political parties.

As Sarkozy explained in *Testimony*, after that first meeting with Chirac, he was with him for every major political battle for the next 15 years. He was there for the creation of Chirac's political party, Rally for the Republic (RPR). He was there when Chirac became mayor of Paris in 1976. He was at his side for the legislative elections of 1978 and his first failed run at the presidency in 1981. (Sarkozy was head of the National

Youth Committee in favor of Chirac's candidacy.) He was with him during his second failed attempt at the presidency in 1988, organizing the main campaign meetings. It is even said that for a time he dated Jacques Chirac's daughter, Claude, whose mother, Bernadette, described Nicolas as the perfect son-in-law.

As Sarkozy took pains to point out in his book *Testimony*, however, he always maintained his political freedom from Chirac and the RPR. He never worked directly for the party, was never a paid employee. As he put it, "working for a party is like being in an intellectual prison, cut off from all freedom of choice . . . material dependence inevitably leads to political dependence. And I wanted to preserve my political freedom at all costs."

Being a political protégé is all well and good, and in some cases necessary, but to gain political freedom, it does become necessary to own one's political position. In 1977, Sarkozy became a member of the Neuilly-sur-Seine municipal council, a position he would hold for six years, with the help and support of the city's mayor, Achille Peretti. Much would happen during that time: he earned his master's degree in 1978 and passed the bar exam in 1981, working as an attorney specializing in business law. By becoming an attorney, Sarkozy felt, he would not have to be dependent on politics for his livelihood. As he said in *Testimony*, "I became a lawyer and I love it. Most important, it gave me the reassurance and the certainty of having a job to fall back on. Without that, I would never have been able to take the risks that I have taken throughout my career. I owe to this profession the independence I've needed to remain a free man. It is so much easier to say no when you know your professional future is secure."

Then, on December 23, 1982, Nicolas Sarkozy got married. Her name was Marie-Dominique Culioli, the daughter of a pharmacist from Vico (a village north of Ajaccio, Corsica). The couple had two sons: Pierre (born in 1985) and Jean (born in 1987). One of the witnesses of the couple's wedding was the prominent right-wing politician Charles Pasqua. Just one year later, he would become one of Sarkozy's first political opponents.

Working on the Neuilly-sur-Seine municipal council, Sarkozy had, as Tim King described in *Prospect* magazine, "worked his way into the entourage of Charles Pasqua, senator and a leader of the party." When Achille Peretti died unexpectedly, Pasqua was obviously next in line to replace him.

Unfortunately for Pasqua though, he had not counted on the ambition of his protégé, Nicolas Sarkozy. While Pasqua was in the hospital for a minor operation, Sarkozy proposed himself for the position of mayor. By the time Charles Pasqua was in a position to do anything about it, Sarkozy had rounded up enough support to be elected.

Pasqua was furious. He was the first, as Tim King put it, "to be stung by Sarkozy's treachery." Sarkozy himself is quoted as saying, "I screwed them all." His partner at the head of the RPR (Rally for the Republic, which had taken the place of the Union of Democrats for the Republic), Jacques Chirac, simply laughed. "Everyone betrays everyone else in this job," was his response, according to Tim King. While Chirac may have gained new respect for Sarkozy's ambition and political ruthlessness, (Chirac himself did not actively support Sarkozy in his move, but he did nothing to stop him either), his feelings would be very different just 12 years later.

For Nicolas Sarkozy, it was the end of the first stage of his political career. As he described in his book *Testimony*, it had been even more difficult than he had imagined:

> My political journey was a lot harder than people have often said and even than I have admitted. A lot of political leaders have found their vocation by working in a ministerial cabinet right after graduating from the National Administration School (ENA). It is much harder to start as a grassroots

Sarkozy's reputation as a ruthless politician began when he became the mayor of Neuilly-sur-Seine. Although Charles Pasqua, a friend and colleague of Sarkozy, was due to inherit the position, he was recovering from surgery when Sarkozy garnered enough support to usurp him. *Above*, Sarkozy's official portrait as mayor.

party organizer and climb your way up, but that's the route I took. I was secretary for my constituency, then regional treasurer, then a leader of my region—I served at practically every basic level possible. It wasn't until ten years after I first started in politics that I became mayor of Neuilly. . . .

Sarkozy, 28 years old, was the youngest mayor ever of any town in France with a population of over 50,000. Through being mayor, he was now in a position where he was able to befriend a number of influential people, including the billionaire Martin Bouygues, whose group owns the TV station TF1, as well as the TV presenter Jacques Martin. Indeed, in his role of mayor, he actually conducted the marriage of the 53-year-old Martin to his bride, the beautiful 27-year-old Cecilia Maria Sara Isabel Ciganer. Little did anyone attending the wedding guess that just five years later, the young bride would leave her husband to live with Nicolas Sarkozy.

Taking a Risk

CECILIA MARIA SARA ISABEL CIGANER (LATER CIGANER-ALBÉNIZ) WAS BORN on November 12, 1957. Her father, Andre Ciganer (née Aron Chouganov) was born of Romanian- and Russian-Jewish origins, although some sources claim that he was a Romanian White Russian émigré of Gypsy-Jewish origins. Born in Bucharest, Romania, in 1898, he left home at the age of 13, just prior to World War I. For 20 years, Andre wandered throughout Europe, holding papers that declared him a "state-less citizen," working odd jobs and romancing his way through life. (In this, he was not unlike Nicolas Sarkozy's own father.)

Cecilia's Spanish-Belgian mother, Teresita "Diane" Albéniz de Swert, was a daughter of the Spanish diplomat Alfonso Albéniz Jordan, and the granddaughter of the Spanish composer Isaac Albéniz i Pascual. Andre and Teresita met on the Basque coast, and just 15 days later, Andre, age 39, asked Teresita, just 18, to marry him.

In the 1940s, Andre and Teresita, who had changed her name to Diane, moved to Paris, where he took a job as a furrier in a shop in the 8th arrondissement. There the couple had four children, three boys and one girl, Cecilia. "Our childhood was calm and rather spoiled," Cecilia recalled in an interview with *Liberation* in 2004. "We never moved and were brought up in the Catholic faith."

Despite her calm upbringing, when Cecilia was a child, she suffered from cardiac problems that slowed down her growth. After undergoing open cardiac surgery at the age of 13, she quickly made up for her growth delay, shooting up to 5'10" (five inches taller than her future husband, Nicolas Sarkozy). She studied piano and obtained a baccalaureate after studying 13 years in a French Catholic school, Soeurs de Lubek. While studying law in Assas, she lived on small jobs, and modeling for fashion designer Elsa Schiaparelli at night. She ended her studies before obtaining her degree, continued modeling, and eventually became a parliamentary assistant to Rene Touzet, a friend of her brother.

She won the attention of the popular TV host Jacques Martin, already two times married and the father of four. She soon became pregnant, and just twelve days before giving birth to her first child, the two married. The couple had two daughters: Judith (born August 22, 1984) and Jeanne-Marie (born June 8, 1987).

The civil wedding was held at the town hall of Neuilly. As required by law, mayors or their deputies oversee marriages, and it was Neuilly's mayor, Nicolas Sarkozy, who was to have the honor. Even though Cecilia was about ready to give birth to another man's daughter, Sarkozy was immediately smitten. "What was I doing, marrying her to another man!" he is quoted as saying by the *Independent*, "I fell in love with her almost immediately. I thought, I must have that woman. She's mine." Undoubtedly though, his wife at the time, Marie-Dominique, would have something to say about that.

Although many sources say that Nicolas and Cecilia did not see each other for three years, when, as Sarkozy put it, he was "struck by lightning" by seeing her again, other sources disagree. They say that the Sarkozys and the Martins actually became friends and even went on ski trips together. According to Nicolas Sarkozy's biographer, Catherine Ney, one day, Marie-Dominique followed her husband's footsteps in the snow. They came to a stop outside of Cecilia's window.

Five years later, after Nicolas had separated from Marie-Dominique, Cecilia left her husband. "I left with my two little darlings (aged four years and six months) under each arm," she later recalled, as quoted in the *Independent*. Cecilia and Nicolas began living together.

One year later, Cecilia had obtained her divorce from Jacques. Nicolas was not so fortunate. Marie-Dominique fought hard to keep her marriage together. Cecilia and Nicolas would not be able to marry until October 23, 1996.

Those years were difficult for the couple. According to the *Independent*, people sometimes referred to her as "the mayor's whore." Cecilia herself said, "Life was hell. Everybody in Neuilly was pointing the finger at us. I was looked down on."

The scandal had little to no effect on Sarkozy's political career, however. Unlike in the United States for example, where President Bill Clinton's relationship with White House intern Monica Lewinsky nearly led to his being driven out of office, the French (along with many other Europeans) have a much more tolerant attitude toward the private lives of their politicians.

As Caroline Wyatt explained for BBC News, the late French president François Mitterrand managed to keep secret a mistress and an illegitimate child for most of his presidency. Jacques Chirac himself has admitted to having loved many women "as discreetly as possible." As Jean-Francois Probst, a long-time advisor for Chirac put it, "The French are very tolerant. They will brush off affairs, they will disregard financial

Throughout his career, Sarkozy's love life has often overshadowed his political decisions. While serving as mayor of Neuilly, the married Sarkozy *(above left)* fell in love with Cecilia Maria Sara Isabel Ciganer *(above right)*. The scandal was splashed all over the newspapers and the couple faced intense public scrutiny.

scandals. . . ." This tolerant attitude, accepting of human weakness, would become invaluable as Sarkozy's career progressed.

CAREER MOVEMENT

In 1988, the same year that Cecilia left her husband for him, Nicolas Sarkozy decided that the time was right to make his next political move. He decided to run for the National Assembly, the principal legislative branch of the French Parliament. Its 577 deputies are directly elected for five-year terms in local majority votes, and every seat is voted on in each election.

Once again taking a political risk, Sarkozy decided to run for Parliament, taking on the incumbent deputy, Florence d'Harcourt. Jacques Chirac had already promised d'Harcourt the support of the RPR, but Sarkozy sensed an opportunity and seized it. He won the election, and, as he said in *Testimony*, "it was only at this time that I began to hold political responsibility alongside Chirac."

In order to understand Sarkozy's role in government and his relationship with Jacques Chirac, it is important to understand how the French government is arranged.

THE GOVERNMENT OF FRANCE

Broadly speaking, France is considered to be a semi-presidential and representative democratic republic. This means that the president of France is the head of state (the chief public representative of the government), while the prime minister of France is the head of government (the chief officer of the executive branch of government, presiding over the cabinet). As a means of comparison, in the United States, the president carries out both roles, being both the head of state and the head of government. In France, the position is divided between two people.

The president is chosen by popular vote and is elected to a five-year term. The president names the prime minister, presides over what is known as the *gouvernement* (cabinet of ministers), directs the armed forces, and concludes treaties. The president may also submit questions to national referendums and can dissolve the National Assembly. All of the president's powers, though, are subject to countersigning (*contreseing*, in French) by the prime minister, except in a few cases, such as dissolving the National Assembly.

In certain emergencies, the president may assume special powers. In normal times, however, the president cannot pass either legislation or regulations. If his party has a majority in Parliament, he may "strongly suggest" the adoption of certain legislation, or request his prime minister to take on such-and-such regulation. In any event, because the president is elected, in theory by at least half of the voting population, he is the dominant figure in French politics.

As previously stated, it is the president who appoints the prime minister. He cannot, however, dismiss him; but if the prime minister is from the same political side, he can, in practice, have him resign on demand. (It is known that prime ministers are asked to sign a non-dated letter of resignation before actually being nominated for the position.) He also appoints the ministers, ministers-delegate, and secretaries. When the president's political party or supporters control Parliament, the president is then the dominant player in executive action, being able to choose whomever he wishes for the government and having it follow his political agenda.

Such dominance is not always the case, however. When, as often happens, the president's political opponents control Parliament, the president's authority can be severely limited, since he must choose a prime minister and cabinet who reflect the majority in Parliament and who will implement the agenda of the parliamentary majority. (It is as if, for example, in the United States, there was a Republican president and a Democratic Congress, that the president would be forced to choose a vice president and cabinet that reflected the Democratic majority.)

When parties from opposite ends of the political spectrum control Parliament and the presidency, the power-sharing arrangement is known as cohabitation. Cohabitation mainly occurred prior to 2002 because at that time the presidential term was for seven years, while Parliament was for five years, which meant that elections were held years apart and support for one party or another could easily change. Now that the presidential term has been shortened to five years and the elections are separated by only a matter of weeks, when public opinion is still relatively unchanged, this is much less likely to happen.

The gouvernement is headed by the prime minister and has at its disposal the civil service, the government agencies, and the armed forces. It is responsible to Parliament, which forces the gouvernement to be from the same political stripe as the majority in the National Assembly. Government ministers cannot pass legislation without the approval of Parliament.

The Parliament itself, the legislative branch, is made up of two houses: the National Assembly and the Senate. The assembly is the preeminent body, made up of 577 deputies directly elected for five-year terms. The National Assembly can force the resignation of the executive cabinet by voting a motion of censure. It is for this reason that the prime minister and his cabinet are by necessity from the dominant party (or coalition, if no one party has a majority) in the assembly.

Parliament passes statutes and votes on the budget. It also exerts control on the actions of the president through questioning on the floor of the houses of Parliament and by establishing commissions of enquiry. The constitutionality of the statutes is checked by the Constitutional Council, whose members are appointed by the president, the president of the National Assembly, and the president of the Senate. Former presidents of the republic are also members of the council.

MEMBER OF THE MINORITY

The parliamentary elections of 1988, the year that Nicolas Sarkozy was first elected to the National Assembly, ended a two-year period of cohabitation in the French government. After the 1986 assembly elections, French president François Mitterrand, a socialist from the left wing of French politics, was forced to nominate as prime minister Jacques Chirac, the leader of the RPR, the largest party in the Parliament's majority coalition. Throughout this cohabitation period, President Mitterrand focused on his foreign duties and allowed Chirac to control internal affairs.

Although Jacques Chirac dominated the RPR, another prominent right-wing politician during this period was Édouard Balladur, the man who developed the very theory of "cohabitation." He held that if the right won the legislative election, it could in fact govern without the resignation of Socialist president Mitterrand. As minister of economy of finance, Balladur sold off a number of public companies and abolished the wealth tax.

This period of cohabitation lasted for just two years, until 1988, when the newly reelected Françoise Mitterrand, feeling confident of his party's popularity, dissolved the Parliament and called for new legislative elections. Mitterrand's confidence was well placed; the elections were won by a leftist majority, which lasted five years. The RPR was now the minority power in the National Assembly.

So from 1988 to 1993, Nicolas Sarkozy found himself as a minority member of the National Assembly, virtually powerless to influence events. He used this time to organize annual meetings of the opposition along with another member of the RPR, Alain Madelin. He also worked tirelessly on the creation of a political platform that could help his party win the 1993 legislative elections.

He found himself growing politically closer to Édouard Balladur. It was, in a way, a new direction for Sarkozy, since, as he described in *Testimony*, "until then, my political repertoire consisted only of power plays, applause lines, ready-made ideas and putting my inexhaustible energy behind Jacques Chirac."

Working with Balladur changed Sarkozy and helped him to develop as a politician. He explained this in *Testimony*, saying,

> . . . I discovered several things: the advantages of compromise, tolerance, respect for skepticism, a profound

commitment to consensus (or at least a strong aversion to conflict), and a healthy detachment from people and events. In short, I felt able to use new forces and to rise to a new level. I was grateful to Balladur for having considered me to be up to crossing this threshold.

When the right won an 80 percent majority in the National Assembly elections of 1993, the French once again had a cohabitation government. President Mitterrand was again forced to appoint an opposition leader to the post of prime minister. Jacques Chirac was unwilling to renew his "cohabitation" relationship with President Mitterrand, so Édouard Balladur was named prime minister. Now, with his mentor Jacques Chirac as head of the RPR, and Édouard Balladur, the new prime minister, Nicolas Sarkozy was forced to make an important political decision.

He was, in a sense, in a position of power. The political platform that he had helped create had been a large factor in the right's victory in the legislative elections. In addition, he had become a prominent media figure, known to the general public for the first time because of his display of courage in negotiations with "the human bomb." For perhaps the first time in his political career, he was in a position to choose, a position to control his own destiny.

His long-time mentor, Jacques Chirac, wanted him to take over from Alain Juppe as secretary-general of the RPR. But at the same that Chirac wanted Sarkozy to take over the party, Édouard Balladur wanted him to join the government as his minister for the budget. Would he follow Chirac's advice, or would he do what his political instincts demanded?

For Sarkozy, it was an easy decision. It was a time to act; he wanted power, he wanted to join the government. "I wanted to join the government so badly that I had no trouble convincing Chirac to accept this, and I entered the government as minister for the budget," he stated in *Testimony*.

MINISTER OF BUDGET

Sarkozy spent the next two years as Balladur's minister for the budget. It was, as he said, his first real taste of power. It was also another learning experience. As he recalled in *Testimony*,

> For two years, I learned and evolved all the more because in government there is always some battle to be waged, some crisis to resolve, or some challenge to meet. I could thus use all my energy, with the only limit being my physical strength. Since not so many of us in government worked like this, I ended up taking on even greater responsibilities than the already significant ones Balladur initially gave me. I was all for it. The prime minister needed me.

Until one actually holds such a position of power, it is next to impossible to know what it is really like. Even though Nicolas Sarkozy had spent life dreaming of having political power, it was, when he finally achieved it, somewhat different than he had imagined.

As he discussed in *Testimony*, going in to office, looking at it from the outside, he had "a superficial and actually rather silly idea about power. Having never had it, I had a sort of immature fascination with it." For the first few weeks in office, Sarkozy relished his new power, and he admitted that he quickly developed a swelled head and elevated opinion about himself, despite warnings he received from friends and family. Just as quickly, though, reality set in, and he learned a few things about power: "I had to accept that power was no fun, and in fact that it was rather sad. The combination of derision and suspicion that people felt about politicians didn't do [a] minister any favors. You've got to fight, withstand criticism, and attack relentlessly, day and night."

In many ways, politics is a combat sport. All the players are relentlessly trying to gain more power, but the quickest way to do that is to attack your opponents, making them

In cohabitation, if a president's political party does not win the majority of seats in Parliament, the president is forced to choose a prime minister from the group with the most representatives in Parliament. Édouard Balladur *(above)*, another influential figure in Sarkozy's political career, developed the theory of cohabitation and later served as prime minister under a president from an opposing party.

your "enemies." A politician is always on alert, waiting for his adversaries to show a weakness that can be exploited and attacked, and always defending himself (something like a game of dodge ball, but with much higher stakes). Decisions often have to be made quickly, without time for serious thought. As Sarkozy described it, "You don't make the necessary decisions, you take shortcuts, and you don't get the serenity you need to exercise power."

Not only that, but once in power, politicians are constantly looking ahead to the next elections. No sooner had the winners of the 1993 legislative elections settled into their positions than the jockeying for position started in preparation for the 1995 presidential elections. This would present a huge dilemma for Nicolas Sarkozy. Prime Minister Édouard Balladur's popularity had grown within the RPR as well as with the public and the media. Jacques Chirac, who held the position of mayor of Paris, was determined to run for president as well. Sarkozy would have to decide which of his two mentors to support. It would be one of the most momentous political decisions he would ever have to make.

BACKING THE WRONG HORSE

Although Sarkozy's natural instinct would be to support Jacques Chirac, he had become more and more impressed with Édouard Balladur the longer he worked with him. He grew to appreciate Balladur's approach to power, the way that his personality reassured people and united them, rather than dividing them. As he said in *Testimony*, "I was working every day, practically every minute, with a prime minister in whom I had confidence and with whom I saw eye to eye on practically everything. How could I not support him?"

By supporting Balladur, however, he would be turning his back on his long-time friend and mentor, Jacques Chirac. In November of 1993, he made the decision to tell Chirac that he would be supporting his rival, Édouard Balladur, for the presidency of France. Chirac did not react well to the decision. "By supporting Balladur like this, you're putting all your eggs in one basket," he warned his young ally. It was Chirac's way of warning his young protégée that if he turned his back on his mentor and backed Balladur, he was risking his political future by losing Chirac's support should Balladur lose—and Chirac

THIS WOULD BE THE LAST SERIOUS CONVERSATION BETWEEN [CHIRAC AND SARKOZY] FOR MORE THAN THREE YEARS.

meant what he said. This would be the last serious conversation between the two men for more than three years.

At the time, though, it seemed unlikely that Balladur would lose. Indeed, just four months before the election, he led Chirac by almost 20 points in the polls. Jacques Chirac never could be written off as a political force, however. Running as an "outsider," he criticized Balladur as the representative of "dominant ideas," and the gap between the two quickly closed. On election day, Balladur received only 18.5 percent of the vote, finishing behind both Chirac and the Socialist candidate, Lionel Jospin. Chirac went on to defeat Jospin in the second round of voting, receiving 52.6 percent of the vote.

Having won the election, Jacques Chirac was in no mood to mend fences or make peace with either Balladur or the politicians who had supported him. Despite the fact that Chirac and Balladur had been friends for 30 years, the episode greatly strained their friendship. The so-called Balladuriens, the followers of Balladur, including Nicolas Sarkozy, were ostracized from the new Chirac administration. Sarkozy's days of power were over, at least for the time being.

LESSONS LEARNED

For Jacques Chirac, the feelings of betrayal ran deep. Nicolas Sarkozy had been more than a political ally. He had dated Chirac's daughter, been his friend, and had, in effect, become part of his family. Chirac, along with his wife and daughter, felt humiliated by someone who had been allowed to cross the line from political ally to friend. Chirac's wife, Bernadette, reportedly said, "He saw us in our night clothes, he was that close to the family. He betrayed us."

Indeed, the feeling of betrayal ran so deep that it is said by many that the relationship between Nicolas Sarkozy and Jacques Chirac never recovered. In an interview with Charlie Rose on January 31, 2007, Sarkozy denied that he had been a traitor and discussed the events of that election:

> Treachery is somebody who doesn't say what they're going to do. I was speaking to him. And I said it to him, face to face. I'm Balladur's minister, I am his spokesman. I will support Balladur if he's a candidate.
>
> Where's the treachery in that? I made a choice. We're free in France, aren't we? Are we not entitled to make such a choice? And Jacques Chirac, didn't he choose when he decided to favor Giscard up in Chaban d'Elmas? He could answer better than anybody else. And then Balladur lost, he was beaten. So I lost. And I dropped right down to the bottom of the ladder, and climbed up rung by rung on my own. Surely that should give rise to respect. There's no ancient rift that still exists. . . . I admire him [Chirac]. I admire his energy. For his extraordinary career. I have respect for his courage.

Sarkozy resented the fact that he was being punished for his decision. As he said in *Testimony*, "For a long time I remained stunned by the reactions and by the length of the penitence expected of me." He felt that since he had been honest and open about his decision, and because, after all, both Chirac and Balladur were from the same political party, that he should have been respected for his courage. Instead, he lost his position as minister for the budget, was out of political favor, and was called a traitor by the new president's supporters. Although still a member of the National Assembly, he was in political exile and would have to "cross the desert" in order to start again.

6

Coming Back

FRENCH POLITICS, LIKE POLITICS IN MANY OTHER COUNTRIES, IS MADE UP of swings in popularity between what is called "the right" and "the left." But what do those terms mean in regard to French politics, and what role does government have in the life of the average French citizen?

Simply put, the government plays a vital role in the life of the average French citizen. Unlike in the United States, where individual interests predominate, in France, the general interest predominates, and it is the responsibility of the government to identify what is best for the general interest and then to defend it.

In France, nearly 30 percent of the people work for what is known as the public sector (state and local authorities, schools, and state-owned companies and utilities). One out of five French families lives in public housing, and employees of state-owned utilities do far better financially than those who work for private firms. Unlike in the United States, where many feel that less government is better government and that people should be able to make it through their own efforts, the French believe that it is the government's responsibility to ensure good social and economic conditions for every citizen.

And, unlike many Americans, most French citizens see the state as a protection against the hazards of life and not as a burden. Indeed everybody on the Left, and even most people on the Right believe strongly in what they call the French *modèle social* (social model). For them, this means that the state helps to provide free or moderately priced services such as health care and education, a decent compensation for the unemployed, and a guaranteed minimum income for all. The role of government is to build a good society.

In the United States, this kind of government would be unacceptable to the right wing of American politics. To the right wing of French politics, it is by and large accepted that the government will continue to play a large role in the lives of its citizens. In a nation with an economy in the doldrums and unemployment in double digits, however, it is also obvious to many on the Right in France that the system needs to be fixed.

The politicians of the Right want to place more emphasis on individual responsibility and to lessen government intervention in the economy. This policy, known as *liberalisme,* would allow the forces of the free market to operate (as they do in the United States) with little or no regulation. The Right believes that these changes would liberate the economy, allowing it to grow much more rapidly, help provide more jobs, and increase the prosperity of all.

The Left opposes these changes. They believe that individual employees are weak in comparison with employers and market forces. Because of this, they believe that government intervention is necessary for their own welfare, and they point out that gains in the rights of workers were historically achieved by government intervention. These two opposing beliefs about the role of government have ruled French politics since the 1980s.

STARTING OVER

Sarkozy believed in the need for radical change. He saw an economy that had stalled, growing unemployment, a loss of initiative, and a reluctance to make what he believed were necessary changes. His dream, as he said in *Testimony*, was to make a "clean break" from the past.

> The clean break I want to see is not a break with the France we love. It is not a break with our ideals, our values of solidarity, our conception of the State, our tradition of openness, or our ambition—so audacious but now so natural—to influence the destiny of the world. The break we need is a break with the old ways of doing things. It's a break with the way we've approached politics for years.

This break would be known as "the rupture." But before it could happen, Nicolas Sarkozy would have to begin making his way back up the political ladder. Ironically, it was Jacques Chirac who helped make it possible.

In 1997, trying to strengthen his party's ruling coalition, Chirac dissolved Parliament and called for early legislative elections. This move was considered quite a political gamble, designed to increase support for his conservative economic program. The gamble failed.

Instead, it created a public uproar, and his power, which he hoped to increase, was weakened by the public backlash. The Socialist Party (PS), joined by other parties on the Left, defeated Chirac's conservative allies, forcing Chirac into a new period of cohabitation with Lionel Jospin as prime minister, a period that would last for five years.

In the wake of the party's defeat, Sarkozy's undeniable skills as a politician could not be overlooked because of a personal

The 1995 presidential elections briefly ended Sarkozy's role in national politics, as his support of Édouard Balladur strained relations with friend and mentor Jacques Chirac *(above right)*. When Chirac was elected president, Sarkozy immediately lost his minister position and was publicly scorned for his betrayal.

grudge. He was called in and made the number two man in the party. Two years later, when party leader Philippe Seguin resigned, Sarkozy took over as head of the RPR. Once again, his career was on the rebound. Once again, however, it would not last.

ELECTIONS FOR THE EUROPEAN PARLIAMENT

On June 13, 1999, elections to the European Parliament were held in France. The European Parliament is the directly elected parliamentary body of the European Union. The European Union, or EU, is a political and economic community comprised of 27 member states.

The EU, which came into being with the Maastricht Treaty in 1993, created a single European market that seeks to guarantee the freedom of movement, people, goods, services, and capital between member states. It maintains a common trade policy, agricultural and fisheries policies, and a regional development policy. Since 1999, the EU has even had a common currency, the euro, which has been adopted by 13 member states. The EU has even developed a role in foreign policy, as well as in justice and home affairs. By uniting together and speaking with one voice (while still maintaining each country's independence and national identity), the countries of Europe have become influential players on the world stage.

When elections were held in France in 1999 to elect French representatives to the European Parliament, it was Nicolas Sarkozy's role to run the campaign for the RPR, hoping to get as many of its roster of candidates elected as possible. It was his first national political campaign, and he hoped for the best, but the closer it got to election day, the worse the polls numbers for his party got.

After six weeks of campaigning, the RPR came in a dismal third place, with 12.82 percent of the vote, winning just 12 seats in Parliament. The left-wing Socialist Party came in first with 21.95 percent of the vote and 22 seats, followed by the dissident Rally for France, a right-wing party opposed to further European integration, headed by Sarkozy's old political rival Charles Pasqua. Rally for France received 13.05 percent of the vote and 13 seats. It was a humiliating result.

At 11:00 P.M. on election night, Sarkozy went to campaign headquarters and made a short statement to the waiting media. Deciding not to mince words, he took the full responsibility for the loss. After doing so, he turned and left, wanting nothing more than to get away from the questioning of the media and go home to his family. It was not to be, though.

He received a call on his cell phone from Jacques Chirac, telling him that his concession speech at campaign headquarters was not enough. "You've got to go on television. You have to make sure you don't give the impression that you're backing down. Take full responsibility!"

Accompanied by Cecilia, he went to the studios of TF1, the national television network. On the drive there, he learned two pieces of good news that, though they did not alter the final results, at least gave him a personal boost. First, he had edged out Charles Pasqua on Pasqua's home turf of Hauts-de-Seine. Second, the voters of Neuilly had stuck by him, giving his list overwhelming support against the one led by the regional governor of Neuilly Nord. At least in his electoral base, among the people who knew him best, he had remained a winner.

He arrived in the studio to be interviewed by Patrick Poivre d'Arvor, one of France's most well-known television interviewers. He described the nerve-wracking scene in *Testimony*:

Looking me in the eyes, he asked me what it felt like to have lost. I didn't see him as acting out of some sort of sick curiosity or even as one of those moving in for the kill. Rather, I took it as an invitation finally to be myself in this human way that people who don't know me rarely see, and which they doubt exists. And indeed, for once, I hadn't prepared, written, or calculated anything. My words came out following the emotions of the moment, without any advance reasoning. At this particular moment, I just didn't care about political calculations or even my appearance,

FAILURE WAS UNDENIABLE . . .
AND I HAD TO PAY THE PRICE.

Nicolas Sarkozy

which I admit has not always been the case. I just spoke the truth, without running away or apologizing, and without making any excuses. Failure was undeniable . . . and I had to pay the price.

And there was a price to pay. Due to his party's poor performance in the European Parliament election, Nicolas Sarkozy stepped down as head of the RPR. Once again, he would have to wait for another turn of events to give him another shot at the top.

He also learned an important lesson about failure. As he said in *Testimony*:

> . . . in dealing with the consequences of failure, you have to learn to think long-term, to maintain the hope of coming back, and to keep your self-confidence up. You can't inspire confidence in others if you don't have faith in yourself. . . . The hardest thing to do is doubtless to see it as an opportunity and a respite—a chance to draw lessons for the future.

With France being governed by the left-wing coalition of Prime Minister Lionel Jospin, Sarkozy had two years to contemplate his losses and to further develop his philosophy on politics and governing. He remained confident that the French people were ready to accept change and that it was possible for the Right to win elections and make change possible. It would just take more time.

2002 PRESIDENTIAL ELECTIONS

At 69 years old, French president Jacques Chirac ran his fourth campaign for the presidency of France in 2002, having lost twice against Mitterrand in 1981 and 1988. It was the first election for which the president would be elected to a five-year, instead of a seven-year, term.

In the period leading up to the election, the campaign had become increasingly centered on the issue of law and order, with a strong emphasis on crimes committed by young people, and especially those crimes committed by young people of foreign origin. Lionel Jospin, the French prime minister, was criticized as being "soft" on crime by his political opponents; others said that the whole issue of crime was overemphasized by an alarmist media. (In France, as in the United States, the media can concentrate so heavily on discussing violent crime that people can become more concerned about crime than actual numbers would indicate they should be.)

The first round of the election came as a shock to many, since most observers had expected the second ballot to be between Jacques Chirac and Lionel Jospin. Jospin's poor showing (he received only 16.18 percent of the vote), combined with a splintering of the vote on the Left meant instead that Jean-Marie Le Pen of the National Front (FN) would face Chirac (who received only 19.88 percent of the vote) in the second round of voting. (In French presidential elections, if no candidate receives a majority of the vote in the first round, the top two candidates face off in a second round of balloting.)

Running against Le Pen virtually guaranteed Chirac's victory. Jean-Marie Le Pen was (and still is) one of the most controversial politicians in France. His party, strongly law and order and strongly anti-immigrant, was considered to be on the fringes of the political scene. Its unexpectedly strong showing stirred national opinion, with more than a million people taking part in street rallies expressing opposition to Le Pen's ideas.

All political parties outside of the National Front called for opposing Le Pen even if it meant voting for Jacques Chirac, who many distrusted after years of accusations of corruption. (Slogans such as "Vote for the crook, not the fascist" appeared

Jacques Chirac *(above, third from left)* was successfully elected to his second term as president, but was forced to ask Sarkozy *(center)* for help during the campaign. Believing he would be named prime minister after the election was over, Sarkozy was instead appointed minister of the interior.

throughout France, similar to the elections for the governorship of Louisiana in 1991. In that election, a former head of the Ku Klux Klan, white supremacist David Duke, ran against Edwin Edwards, a man who also faced numerous charges of corruption. Bumper stickers popped up throughout the state, saying, "Vote for the Crook, It's Important.") Chirac won the May 5 election in a landslide, winning 82 percent of the vote. (Edwards won his election as well.)

Chirac's winning streak continued for the French legislative elections, held on June 9 and 16, 2002. After the presidential elections, in order to prepare for the legislative elections, the three right-wing parliamentary parties united as one in the Union for the Presidential Majority in order to bring together all of Chirac's supporters in one organization. The UMP went on to win the election, earning a parliamentary majority of 394 seats. Five months later it became the Union for a Popular Movement (UMP), which today is the main French center-right political party.

What was Sarkozy's role in the election? In 2001, he had written a book, *Libre* ("Free"), that made clear his political beliefs. The book did well, and that, combined with Sarkozy's continuing popularity within the RPR, forced Chirac to turn to Sarkozy for support. Chirac made it clear that he despised Sarkozy but needed him as well; "*indispensable mais insupportable*" ("*indispensable but insupportable*") he reportedly said. It is also said that a deal was made. If Sarkozy would help Chirac get re-elected, there was an excellent possibility that Chirac, in turn, would name Sarkozy as the new prime minister.

Sarkozy, a tireless campaigner, traveled through France virtually non-stop, using his political influence to gain as many votes for Chirac as possible. Even though Chirac won the election, however, he did not name Sarkozy as prime minister. Instead he gave the position to Jean-Pierre Raffarin, offering Sarkozy the position of minister of the interior. According to the *Carnad Enchaine*, Sarkozy did not take the news well. "He smashed nearly everything in the office," said a witness. "I'd never seen him like that. He was shouting, hurling files at the floor."

Yet in his book *Testimony*, Sarkozy remembered things slightly differently:

> After the President of the Republic chose Jean-Pierre Raffarin as prime minister, I accepted the responsibility of becoming minister of the interior. Truth be told I was

not really disappointed not to have been named prime minister, as I already doubted the president would offer me the job. Jacques Chirac fought the campaign to win and he won. He wanted to govern. To name me would have meant sharing power, and that's not his style. On the other hand, I wanted to take part in what the new government was going to do.

Once again, Nicolas Sarkozy had worked his way back to a position of power. This time, however, he was determined to make it last and do his best for his country. How he did as minister of the interior would determine his political future once and for all.

7

Nearing the Top

WHAT ARE THE RESPONSIBILITIES OF THE MINISTER OF THE INTERIOR? IN THE United States, the secretary of the interior is the head of the United States Department of the Interior, overseeing such agencies as the Bureau of Land Management, the United States Geological Survey, and the National Park Service. Is it the same thing in France? Hardly.

It is actually one of the most important French governmental cabinet positions. The minister, in essence, is responsible for the general "interior security" of the country, whether it be criminal acts or natural catastrophes. He is in charge of law enforcement, the granting of identity documents (passports, identity cards), and relations between the central and local governments. Given the nation's concerns with law and order as well as with immigration, it was a position guaranteed to be in the center of the nation's and the media's attention.

Sarkozy relished the opportunity, saying in *Testimony* that,

> The French wanted action and this ministry needed major
> reform. . . . Moreover, the Interior Ministry is real life—its
> tragedies and passions, which come knocking constantly at
> your door, day and night: hostage taking, terrorist threats,
> forest fires, protests, rave parties, avian flu, floods, disap-
> pearances. . . it's a heavy responsibility. Not a week goes by
> when you don't have to make and take responsibility for
> difficult decisions.

For a man like Nicolas Sarkozy, ambitious, eager to bring about
change, and equally eager to receive publicity, it was an ideal
position.

As minister of the interior, Sarkozy had to deal with a wide
range of issues, from the use of traffic cameras to terrorism
to immigration. He worked tirelessly, and by the end of the
year, he was already making a huge impact, as described by Jon
Henley in the British newspaper the *Guardian*:

> The extraordinary ascension and ever-soaring popularity of
> the hard-hitting interior minister Nicolas Sarkozy ("Speedy"
> to his multitudinous fans) has been the biggest surprise of
> the first few post-electoral months in France since the cen-
> tre-right government swept to power last June.
>
> Diminutive, pugnacious, plain-speaking but somehow
> always human, the former barrister is everywhere. Hours
> after a meeting in London with his British opposite num-
> ber, David Blunkett, with whom he successfully negotiated
> the closure of the Sangatte refugee camp, he was in a small
> town outside Lyon to denounce as an "assassin" the speeding
> driver who killed five volunteer firemen.
>
> A couple of days later, he announced in front of a large
> Parisian department store the deployment of 1,000 extra
> policemen to counter the threat of terrorism over the

HE ALSO WAS CRITICIZED FOR PUTTING FORTH LEGISLATION THAT WAS SEEN BY MANY AS AN INFRINGEMENT ON CIVIL RIGHTS AND THAT SEEMED AIMED LARGELY AT DISADVANTAGED, HEAVILY IMMIGRANT SEGMENTS OF THE POPULATION.

Christmas period. At roughly the same time, a plane was taking off from Charles de Gaulle airport carrying back to Bucharest the first of the illegal Romanian immigrants that [Sarkozy] has had deported. . . .

With every political hot potato in his lap—crime, immigration . . . terrorism, road safety, prostitution—he deals frankly, decisively and above all energetically. He has had a rule: never to let a single day go by without making a visit to somewhere or an announcement about something sensitive. As a result he is never out of the papers for longer than 24 hours.

By the beginning of 2004, according to polls, Nicolas Sarkozy was perhaps the most polarizing politician in France; considered to be both the most popular and also the least popular conservative politician in France, he was obviously a man who was either loved or hated. His "tough on crime" policies, which included increasing the police presence on the streets, a policy of zero tolerance for such crimes as swearing at a policeman, and introducing monthly crime performance ratings, were popular with some and unpopular with others.

He also was criticized for putting forth legislation that was seen by many as an infringement on civil rights and that seemed aimed largely at disadvantaged, heavily immigrant segments of the population. Sarkozy had nothing but scorn for those who opposed such legislation, saying that "Human rights should be first and foremost about the victims."

Although Sarkozy is often painted in the press as being a strict law-and-order politician who is strongly opposed to immigration, the reality is more complex than that. Throughout his career, he has tried to help ease the sometimes tense relationship between the general French population and the rapidly growing Muslim community. Unlike the Catholic Church or Protestants within France who have official leaders and organizations that communicate directly with the government, the Muslim community lacked a structure or voice that could legitimately deal with the government on its behalf.

Sarkozy felt that such an organization was vital to healthy relations between the French government and its Muslim citizens. He supported the foundation in May 2003 of the private nonprofit Conseil Français du Culte Musulman (French Council of the Muslim Faith), an organization meant to represent French Muslims. In addition, Sarkozy suggested amending the 1905 law on the separation of church and state, mostly in order to be able to finance mosques and other Muslim institutions with the use of public funds, in part so that they are less reliant on money from outside of France.

Policies such as those made it harder for critics to paint Sarkozy in simple brushstrokes of black and white. His views and politics were more complex than that. He also was attacked for being too ambitious, for trying to do too much too fast. He talked about that in *Testimony*:

> During the months following my arrival at the interior ministry, I was criticized for going too fast, for going too far, and even being too much. . . . I was too aggressive, too ambitious, too hungry. And it's true, I love life. I love it so much that I've always been surprised by those who advise me to "take my time." As if time were ours to take and you could modulate it as you like. For them, it was always too

soon for me, even if it would soon be too late! I have seen so many people who, by waiting, never did anything at all, that I've been inspired by their example to do the exact opposite. I would rather take risks by daring to do things than regret that I was not able to seize the opportunity when it was there.

Though Nicolas Sarkozy has nothing but praise for the *idea* of ambition, he denies that he is more ambitious than others. As he said in an interview with Michael Denisot in 1995, "... because, truthfully, I am not more ambitious than the others, at least not those who are doing the same job I am. Only I have chosen not to negate this part of myself that has always driven me to move forward, to try to achieve for myself, to exist."

His ambitions, though, were becoming obvious. If anyone doubted whether Sarkozy planned to run for the presidency in 2007, those doubts were dispelled when he was asked in a television interview in 2003 if he ever thought during his morning shave of becoming president one day. "I do, and not just when I shave," Sarkozy replied.

Jacques Chirac, alarmed at Sarkozy's growing popularity, and still harboring mixed feelings about his one-time protégé, decided to remove him from the Ministry of the Interior. In a cabinet reshuffle on March 31, 2004, Sarkozy was moved to the position of finance minister. According to Tim King in *Prospect* magazine, the move was designed to cause Sarkozy to fail. The nation's finances were in such disarray that any moves Sarkozy would make in his new position would alienate him from a large bloc of the populace.

Why would Chirac make such a move? Again, according to Tim King, Chirac did not want Sarkozy to become president. The two men had had too many disagreements, and there was too much personal baggage between the two: "'You've crossed the yellow line,' the president reportedly warned in an exchange quoted by the [satirical newspaper] *Canard Enchainé*, to which Sarkozy replied: 'Chirac hasn't even noticed that for the last ten years yellow lines on roads have been replaced by white: he is from another generation.'"

MINISTER OF FINANCE

If Jacques Chirac had tried to set Sarkozy up in a position that was doomed to failure, however, Sarkozy was equally determined to avoid the trap. As finance minister, he introduced a number of policies that only served to strengthen his position and popularity with both the business community and with the general public.

These were decisions and policies that could not clearly be defined as *liberalisme*, (a hands-off approach to running the government) or *dirigisme* (the traditional French state intervention in the economy.) He approved and oversaw the reduction of the percentage of government ownership in France Telecom from 50.4 percent to 41 percent, while at the same time backing a partial nationalization of the French engineering company Alstom to help the company avoid bankruptcy. He also reached an agreement with the major French retail chains to work together to lower prices on household goods by an average of 2 percent.

After nearly eight months as minister of finance, Sarkozy's popularity was higher than ever. As a result, when party elections were held within the Union for a Popular Movement, he was chosen as the party's new leader, receiving 85 percent of the vote. For the first time since 1976, Jacques Chirac had lost control of his own party.

Chirac would not take his defeat sitting down. After the party elections, he issued a declaration, stating that no one could simultaneously serve as party leader and government minister. To the surprise of many, Sarkozy chose the party, and as Christopher Caldwell said in the *Weekly Standard*, "turned it into a vehicle for promoting his political fortunes."

Concerned about Sarkozy's growing popularity and ambition, President Jacques Chirac demoted his minister of the interior by transferring him to finance department. Many expected Sarkozy to stumble or fail as the new minister of finance, but he was able to implement new policies that helped the government. *Above*, Finance Minister Sarkozy visits a nuclear power plant in central France.

RETURN TO THE INTERIOR

Sarkozy was out of office for only a few months. When France became the first country to vote to reject the proposed European constitution, it was seen as a personal defeat for Jacques Chirac. He had gambled a great deal of his political capital in an effort to win a "Yes" vote, and worse, the defeat was attributed in part to a pair of disastrous television appearances Chirac had made personally promoting the proposal. Forced to make major changes in his government, Chirac appointed Dominique de Villepin, formerly foreign minister, as the new prime minister. Sarkozy was renamed minister of the interior on June 2, 2005, but this time he was allowed to maintain his position as head of the UMP. It was a huge political victory for Sarkozy. His biggest challenges, however, one political, one personal, were just ahead.

With unemployment high and the dream of a better life a remote possibility, unrest had been steadily building among the juvenile population in France. On October 27, 2005, two teenagers, Zyed Benna and Bounna Traore, living in the working-class commune of Clichy-sous-Bois in the eastern suburbs of Paris, were chased by the police. Attempting to escape, they hid in a power substation, where they were electrocuted.

This event triggered riots across France that garnered worldwide attention. While the riots at first were limited to the Paris area, the unrest quickly spread to other areas of the Île-de-France region, then spread through the outskirts of France's urban areas, along with some rural areas as well. By the third of November, it had spread to other cities in France, affecting all 15 of the large *aires urbaines* (statistical regions made up of a commuter belt around a contiguous urban core). Every night, cars and other vehicles were burned, power stations were attacked, and the violence spread.

On November 8, President Jacques Chirac declared a state of emergency, but the violence continued until finally dwindling out by November 16. As a result of 20 nights of rioting, nearly 9,000 vehicles were burned and close to 3,000 people were arrested. It was the worst rioting that France had seen since 1968.

For Nicolas Sarkozy, who had staked out a position as being tough on crime and restoring law and order, his response to the riots would have major implications regarding his presidential aspirations. Any action by Sarkozy was likely to be attacked by his political opponents as well as by members of his political coalition who also might see themselves as potential candidates for the presidency. Sarkozy also remained mindful of Jean-Marie Le Pen and his National Front, who could be counted on to use the riots for their own political gain.

After the fourth night of riots, Sarkozy declared a zero-tolerance policy toward urban violence and announced that 17 companies of riot police and 7 mobile police squadrons would be stationed in troubled Paris neighborhoods. Sarkozy's calls for greater police action were criticized by politicians on the Left, who felt that the government should go after the root causes of the rioting, with greater public funding for housing, education, and job creation.

Sarkozy disagreed with his critics, as he explained in his book *Testimony*, "It was said that the riots were mostly a 'social' protest; that most of the rioters were primarily victims; and that the guiltiest party of all was the State broadly defined, because it hadn't done enough, spent enough, or provided enough education, training, or assistance."

Sarkozy did not accept those arguments. He argued back that the state had spent billions in the suburbs, that it had put dozens of plans in place. Not only did nothing change, things had gotten worse. He argued that the problem was unregulated immigration. He said in *Testimony* that "many of the current problems of our suburbs are the result of unchecked, and therefore poorly managed, immigration." Nicolas Sarkozy sees illegal immigration as a threat to France, as something that must be controlled and regulated.

He also argues that his positions on immigration are often caricatured. He is portrayed as a xenophobe, one who is afraid or contemptuous of foreigners. Sarkozy believes that his position has been oversimplified, saying in *Testimony*,

> For example, I call on State authorities to do more to integrate young people of immigrant backgrounds, so that ethnic communities don't turn inward because of the State's failure, and I'm accused of promoting ethnic divisions. I propose for the first time in years a tailored immigration policy, meaning one that explicitly recognizes the benefits of openness for a country such as France, and they accuse me of encouraging extreme nationalism.
>
> I comment that no one is required to remain in France, that when someone is welcomed somewhere they must respect and if possible love those who welcome them, and I'm accused of xenophobia.

Sarkozy has taken a strong stance on the subject of immigration, however, telling Charlie Rose in 2007,

> It's an enormous problem. What happened in the suburbs is partly a result of uncontrolled immigration policy. I don't believe in zero immigration, but I don't believe that we can accept everybody. Too many people were allowed in the country. They were not adequately integrated, and we had the problems that we had in November 2005 in a certain number of areas where it was—what was reigning was the community law rather than the republic. That's my first comment.
>
> Now, as regards of the measures. Most of the Muslims in France love France and have values that are compatible with those of the republic, but what I say is I do not want Islam in France. I want an Islam of France. And that's not the same thing at all. . . .
>
> In other words, Islam that respects the values of France. Let me give you an example. If you want to come to France,

MANY CRITICS EXPRESSED THE BELIEF THAT IT WAS SARKOZY'S OWN HARSH WORDS THAT CONTRIBUTED TO BOTH THE INTENSITY AND LONGEVITY OF THE RIOTS.

[if] someone wants to come to France, [then] I expect people to respect and love France. If you don't, then you have no reason to be here. . . .

France is a country that's open. But I want people to respect France and respect our rules. I created the French Council for the Muslim Faith, because I don't want imams who don't speak French and I don't want any mosques that are paid for from abroad. I want the Muslims in France to be able to pray freely and in dignity. . . . You can't have a situation where you come to France, you're allowed to come to France and do whatever you like. You can't say I have rights, but I have no obligations.

Despite his words of reassurance, many believed, and still believe, that Sarkozy has strongly negative feelings against immigrants. Sometimes his choice of words bolsters that belief: Prior to the riots he had called for the suburbs to be "cleaned with a Karcher," a reference to a common brand of high-pressure industrial hose, and in a well-publicized incident during the riots, he referred to the rioters as "scum." His remarks were criticized by many on the Left as well as by a member of his own government, Azouz Begag, delegate minister for equal opportunities. Indeed, many critics expressed the belief that it was Sarkozy's own harsh words that contributed to both the intensity and longevity of the riots. He later explained his choice of words in an interview with Charlie Rose:

The term *scum*, well, I arrived there in Argenteuil, it was half past 10:00 in the evening. There were some 200 highly excited people there, insulting us, throwing stones and what have you. It was a tense situation. And in the next couple of hours, there was a fight between the police and these people. And I didn't run off. I stayed there.

And once the police regained control, I went out into the street again. And there were these tower blocks and all the lights were on in the apartments. There was a lady on the first floor who called out to me. And it must have been about midnight or 1:00 in the morning. Mr. Sarkozy, Mr. Sarkozy, she called. And I said, yes, yes that's me. She opened her window. She was a North African lady. And she said to me, Mr. Sarkozy, get rid of the scum. And I said, I'm there precisely for that, to get rid of the scum for you. I use the same term as that of the lady.

Of course, Sarkozy denied meaning that the rioters were actually "scum," saying,

No. There are honest people who live there in that area, in that district. The people who threw stones at the police and burned the buses, that's not good, they're not good people. I stayed there and I discussed things with them. . . . I want to hold a hand out to somebody who wants to improve his lot, but there are certain things I'll never accept.

AFTERMATH

Many political analysts speculated that Sarkozy's angry response to the rioters was, in part, a tactic designed to help collect votes in the upcoming presidential race. They argued that as public fear of immigrant rioters increased, so did the bloc of voters attracted to Sarkozy's tough stance on violence and stricter immigration rules.

Indeed, Sarkozy's popularity did rise, as voters, even those who might normally have been drawn to the extremism of Jean-Marie Le Pen's National Front, saw Sarkozy as the man

One of Sarkozy's biggest challenges was overcoming a wave of violent riots that swept through France's suburbs in 2005. Sarkozy received scathing criticism for his handling of the situation, which he blamed on unrestricted immigration and the lack of integration among different communities. *Above*, a French student protests government actions during the riots by holding a caricature of Sarkozy as Napoleon.

who could and would protect France from the rioting Muslim immigrants. Ironically though, when the riots had ended and investigations began, it became apparent that Islam itself had little to do with the riots.

As the *New York Times* reported, France's most influential Islamic group issued a religious edict, or fatwa, that condemned the violence. "It is formally forbidden for any Muslim seeking divine grace and satisfaction to participate in any action that blindly hits private or public property or could constitute an attack on someone's life."

Indeed, the head of the Direction Centrale des Renseignements Généraux (the intelligence service for the French police) found no Islamic factors in the riots, and the BBC summarized that the reasons behind the events included unemployment among young people and lack of opportunities in France's poorest communities. The *New York Times* again went on to report that "while a majority of the youths committing the acts are Muslim, and of African or North African origin," local residents say that "second-generation Portuguese immigrants and even many children of native French have taken part." These reports largely came too late, as the idea of Muslim riots became firmly entrenched in the minds of much of the French population.

PERSONAL PROBLEMS

Nicolas Sarkozy came out of the riots in an even stronger political position than before, having strengthened his credentials with the French public as a politician who would be strong on law and order. At the same time, though, his personal life was going through a difficult period.

In 2005, Cecilia Sarkozy left her husband and began a very public affair with executive Richard Attias. The relationship became the talk of France as the couple traveled from Cannes and on to New York City, leaving the Sarkozys' son, Louis, in his father's charge. Nicolas Sarkozy was heartbroken.

As he said in *Testimony*, "I never could have imagined going through something like this. I never could have imagined being so devastated." The entire experience of being abandoned left him, as he put it, "profoundly shaken." As reported in the *Sunday Times*, a senator in Sarkozy's own political party remembered seeing him shortly after Cecilia went to live in

New York with Attias. "He sat there eating chocolates, one after the other, not focusing on anything. He was a mess."

Besides the personal pain, there were the political ramifications to think of as well. While the French are relatively tolerant when male politicians have affairs, the reaction is very different when it is the man's wife who is having an affair. As one political commentator said in the *Telegraph*, "Nearly all of our successful male politicians have a history of affairs and divorces. François Mitterrand had a long-standing mistress and this was seen as evidence of his masculinity—his virility, if you like. For Sarkozy, it's the very opposite."

It seemed likely that the couple's difficulties could damage Sarkozy's political ambitions. Indeed, there were some, including Sarkozy himself, who felt that Jacques Chirac's people were involved in leaking information to the media regarding the Sarkozys' marital difficulties, in an effort to harm Nicolas's chances at becoming president.

It was a political loss for Sarkozy in other ways as well. As a PR consultant, Cecilia Sarkozy had had a major influence on creating Nicolas's public image and in helping to direct his political strategy. She had become perhaps his closest advisor, the one that he could most rely on for honest advice. Cecilia alone could help him control his temper and help him to project a warmer, more human image.

The media, as might be expected, had a field day reporting Cecilia Sarkozy's new relationship, but Sarkozy did what he could to fight back. According to some reports, when *Paris Match* published photos of Cecilia and her lover on the front page, Nicolas Sarkozy had his friend Arnaud Lagardere, the owner of the magazine, fire the editor.

In another instance, Valerie Domain, a respected Paris journalist, had written a biography of Cecilia Sarkozy with her cooperation. In November of 2005, however, Cecilia told *Le Parisien* newspaper that she had changed her mind, saying "When I found out the book was about to be published, I called Nicolas urgently. I asked him to help. I told him about it and he said he'd deal with it." Sarkozy, in the midst of the riots, called the publisher to his office and told him, according to the *Telegraph*, "I do not want this book to exist." Within a short period of time, the book's entire first run of 25,000 copies was destroyed, causing French humorist Laurant Requier to remark, as quoted in *New Internationalist*, "If the suburban youth had burned down that warehouse [where the books were stored], Sarkozy would have given them a bonus."

During their period of estrangement, Nicolas Sarkozy did what he could to win his wife back, while at the same time reportedly having a relationship with a journalist of *Le Figaro*, Anne Fulda. In February of 2006, however, in a scene that could have come from a classic romantic movie, Cecilia left her lover and ran down the steps of her airplane and straight into Nicolas's waiting arms. Their dramatic reunion sent Sarkozy's popularity higher, proving that even the French cannot resist a happy ending.

In his book *Testimony*, Sarkozy wrote a moving testimony to his abiding love for Cecilia:

> C. I write *C.* because still today, nearly twenty years after we first met, it moves me to pronounce her name. C. is Cecilia. C. is my wife. She is part of me. Whatever challenges we have faced as a couple, not a day has gone by that we didn't talk. Really! We didn't want to betray anyone, but we're incapable of being apart. It's not that we haven't tried, but it's impossible. We finally realized that it was vital for us to speak to each other, listen to each other, and see each other. . . .
>
> Today, Cecilia and I have gotten back together for real, and surely forever.

Yet, with the riots over and his marriage apparently back on solid ground, other problems arose. Stories began to appear in the press that suggested that Nicolas Sarkozy was corrupt.

This seemed nearly impossible to believe, because, somewhat unusually for a French politician on the center-right, Sarkozy's reputation has always been spotlessly clean. The stories, though, would have to be quickly disproved before the public began to believe them.

According to John Lichfield writing for the *Independent*, the allegations of corruption were traced back to a friend of Prime Minister Dominique de Villepin, Jacques Chirac's ally. De Villepin absolutely denied any attempts to hurt Sarkozy, even though it is said that he refers privately to Sarkozy as "the dwarf." Regardless, Sarkozy emerged from the controversy with his reputation for incorruptibility intact. Another hurdle on his way to the presidency had been cleared.

SETTING THE STAGE

As early as September of 2005, well before riots erupted throughout the nation, Sarkozy had begun to lay out his vision for the future. In an interview with *Le Figaro*, he claimed that the French had been misled for 30 years by false promises, and he denounced what he considered to be unrealistic policies.

He called for a simplified and fairer system of taxation, with fewer loopholes and a maximum taxation rate of 50 percent of revenue. Taking a direct attack on the modèle social français, he approved measures that reduced or even denied social support to unemployed workers who refused work that was offered to them. Finally, he pressed for a reduction in the budget deficit, claiming that the French state had been living off credit for too long.

These policies are what are known in France as *liberal*. (Of course, in the United States, the word *liberal* is used to identify policies of the Left, not of the Right.) Sarkozy himself rejects the term, preferring to be called a pragmatist. This struggle between liberalisme, an opposition to government intervention in the economy, versus dirigisme, a belief in strong governmental control of the economy, was one of the main themes of the 2007 presidential campaign.

There were, of course, other issues that would play prominent roles in the presidential election. As NPR illustrated in a May 14, 2007, Web article, the main areas key to his campaign were

- **Employment:** Work is one of the primary values of Sarkozy's life and was perhaps the centerpiece of his campaign. He claimed to be the candidate of those who get up early to go to work, and that he would reestablish the value of work.
- **Thirty-five-hour work week:** Unlike the United States, which has a 40-hour work week, in the year 2000, the French adopted the 35-hour working week. (Any time worked over 35 hours is considered overtime.) The reason for this was to help reduce unemployment (by having people work fewer hours, companies would, in theory, hire more people to make up for the missing hours) and to give workers more personal time to enhance the quality of their lives. Sarkozy considered the bill to be a huge mistake. While he vowed not to repeal the law, he did want to encourage people to work longer and earn more. He also promised to cut taxes and red tape in order to encourage employment.
- **Immigration:** Sarkozy promised to restrict immigration, to quickly deport illegal immigrants, and to require that all immigrants speak French. Sarkozy also proposed the creation of a new ministry to deal specifically with questions of immigration and nationality— and to grant non-citizens the right to vote. In addition, and not without controversy, he has spoken about the need for affirmative action to help immigrants improve their lives and leave the overcrowded ghettos

that fueled the riots. This would be a major change for the French, who have historically prided themselves on officially treating everyone equally, to the point where minorities are not even identified as such. Sarkozy argues that reality is slightly different, saying that "the reality of our system is that it protects those who have something and it is very tough on those who don't." His proposed policy of affirmative action, or as it became known in France, "positive discrimination," would help make it easier for those living outside the system to enter into French society.

- **Foreign policy:** Sarkozy is a strong friend of Israel. He also has spoken out against the European community offering membership to Turkey, telling Charlie Rose that "Turkey is not in Europe. Turkey is Asia Minor. There's absolutely no reason why Asia Minor should be part of Europe . . . . Turkey is a very great civilization, but it's not a European one. Why should we build Europe with countries that are not European?"

- **Relations with America:** Over the past few years, relations between France and the United States have been strained, largely because of France's lack of support for the Iraq War. While Sarkozy opposes the war, he has a great deal of admiration for America and wants to help improve ties between the two countries. Sarkozy wrote in the preface of his book *Testimony*, "France's friendship with the United States is an important and lasting part of its history. I stand by this friendship, I'm proud of it, and I have no intention of apologizing for feeling an affinity with the greatest democracy in the world."

- **Crime:** As the law-and-order candidate, Sarkozy vowed to be "tough on crime," to impose minimum jail sentences for repeat offenders, and to introduce tougher sentences for juveniles.

It is interesting to realize that based on these positions and others, Nicolas Sarkozy has been accused of being an "ultraliberal," which translates to "ultraconservative" in the French political system. He has been accused of wanting to destroy the modèle social français and let market forces work their magic. He has been called "an American poodle" and a "Bush boy" (referring to George W. Bush). As John Lichfield points out in the April/May 2007 *Bookforum*, however, by American standards his positions would fit in nicely along with those of the Democratic Party:

> Yes, he wants to roll back the French state (which uses 55 percent of the annual GDP). Yes, he wants to cut back on the vast army of 5.2 million French state employees (one in twelve of the population). Yes, he wants to reduce taxes and clamp down on violent youth crime. Yes, he wants to circumscribe the rights of trade unions, especially the right to strike. But he also believes in state intervention to protect, or boost, strategic industries, from energy to pharmaceuticals. He believes in a Gallic version of affirmative action and in European trade preference in some areas (in other words, EU trade barriers against the rest of the world). He believes that politicians, not just bankers, should have a say in the running of the euro. If anything . . . Sarkozy has moved his pieces even closer to the center of the left-tilted political chessboard in France.

Even if his politics were not easily defined as "right" or "left," as both his allies and critics believe, Sarkozy's support among the members of the Union for a Popular Movement was overwhelming. On January 14, 2007, Nicolas Sarkozy was chosen by his party to be its candidate in the 2007 presidential elections. Running unopposed, he won 98 percent of the votes. With his party unified behind him, he would go into the elections with guaranteed support of country's right wing.

His opponents on the Left would not be so lucky. A struggle to lead the Socialist Party erupted between Ségolène Royal, Dominique Strauss-Kahn, and Laurent Fabius. Royal, who ran on a platform of reform, taking consultations with citizens through her Web site, was chosen on November 17, 2006, to lead her party in the presidential election, receiving 60.6 percent of the vote.

Royal, president (state governor) of the Poitou-Charentes region and former member of the National Assembly, was the first woman to represent a major French party in a presidential contest. A populist who promised to raise state pensions, increase the minimum wage, raise benefits for handicapped citizens, and to help provide a job or job training to every student within six months of graduation, campaigned on family and socially oriented issues, rather than economic or foreign policy issues.

The personal life of Royal drew nearly as much attention as that of Sarkozy. From the late 1970s, she was the "private life-partner" of François Holland, with whom she had four children. It has been said that Holland, currently head of the French Socialist Party, had plans to run for president of France, until Royal pushed him aside, gaining her party's nomination. An attractive, charismatic woman, she was often criticized for being stronger on rhetoric and promises than on actual policies, and of being part of a growing trend in French politics to focus on the personality and lifestyle of politicians rather than their ideas.

There were two other leading candidates as well: François Bayrou was the candidate of the centrist Union for French Democracy, and once again, Jean-Marie Le Pen ran for the National Front, promoting policies of strong law enforcement, economic protectionism, and stringent measures to control immigration. One potential candidate who would not be running was French president Jacques Chirac. Facing growing unpopularity, on March 11, 2007, he announced that he would not seek a third term as France's president.

While not endorsing any candidate during that speech, he did devote several minutes of the talk to making a plea against extremist politics. This was considered by many to be a thinly disguised message to voters not to vote for Jean-Marie Le Pen and a recommendation to Sarkozy not to strike themes similar to Le Pen in an attempt to win over his voters. Two weeks later, on March 21, Jacques Chirac, somewhat half-heartedly, announced his support for his one-time protégée, Nicolas Sarkozy.

"Five years ago, I called for the creation of the UMP to allow France to pursue a rigorous policy of modernization," he said, as quoted in the *International Herald Tribune.* "In all its diversity, this political movement chose to support Nicolas Sarkozy in the presidential election, because of his qualities. Naturally, I will therefore bring him my vote and my support." Sarkozy showed his appreciation for the endorsement in a written statement, saying, "I am very touched by this decision. It is important for me on a political but also on a personal level."

It is important to remember that, along with the long simmering personal differences between Chirac and Sarkozy, there were profound political differences as well, with the two men offering very different visions for France's future. Chirac believes that France and Germany together should be the "leaders" of a strong Europe that counterbalances American power. Sarkozy is much more interested in working with the United States. Chirac has always been a strong believer in the French social model. Sarkozy insists that the system needs to be fixed and that changes to the system are inevitable.

At the same time that Chirac made his endorsement, he announced that Sarkozy would step down as minister of the interior on March 26, which would allow him to devote himself full time to the campaign. He would need all the time he could get.

At that point in the campaign, Sarkozy had a narrow lead in the polls for the first round of elections to be held on April 22, less than one month later. His rivals on the Left went strongly on the attack, accusing Sarkozy of being a "candidate for brutality" and for promoting ideas that were too conservative, too right wing for France. "Tout Sauf Sarkozy," or "Anybody but Sarkozy," was their battle cry. One magazine described him as "in some manner mad, and fragile." A former minister, Azouz Begag, alleged that in November 2005, Sarkozy called him on his cell phone, saying "I'm going to smash your face in," after the two disagreed over the way to handle the 2005 riots.

Yet, at the same time, Sarkozy was being attacked by the extreme Right as well. Just days before the first round of elections, Jean-Marie Le Pen spoke out against Sarkozy, insinuating that he was not "French enough" to be president. "Mr. Sarkozy, the world does not revolve around your little person," Le Pen said, as quoted in the *New York Times*. "Long before your parents came from Hungary or Greece, there was at the heart of the French people a national current that cared more about the interests of the country than about its ruling class."

Finding himself being attacked from both sides, and the target of an anti-Sarkozy movement that defaced his political posters by giving his face either a Hitler-like mustache or Dracula's fangs, Sarkozy fought back. In a political rally in Marseilles, he answered his critics. Described by the *New York Times* as " . . . arm chopping in the air, his fists clenched, his face bathed in sweat during a speech before 20,000 supporters, he dismissed the attacks of his opponents, saying he had been singled out because he dared to speak out on tough items like crime, immigration, national identity and the need for authority."

"When candidates have no ideas, no arguments, no convictions, when they believe in nothing," he said, they "have no

> ## "I WANT TO BE THE PRESIDENT WHO WILL MAKE A NEW FRENCH DREAM LIVE, THANKS TO WHICH EVERY FRENCH PERSON WILL LOOK TO THE FUTURE NOT AS A THREAT, BUT AS PROMISE."
>
> —Nicolas Sarkozy

other option than insult, lies and insinuation." He went on to quote Martin Luther King Jr.'s "I have a dream" speech, saying "I want to be the president who will make a new French dream live, thanks to which every French person will look to the future not as a threat, but as promise."

RESULTS AND ROUND TWO

The first round of the election took place on April 22, 2007. Nicolas Sarkozy came in first with 31.18 percent of the votes, comfortably ahead of Ségolène Royal of the Socialists with 25.87 percent. Voter turnout was extraordinarily high, with 85 percent of eligible voters coming out to vote. (This compares with just 64 percent of eligible voters that turned out for the 2004 United States presidential election.) The two remaining candidates, Nicolas Sarkozy and Ségolène Royal, now had just two weeks until the second-round election on May 6.

The two candidates crisscrossed the country, trying to drum up support. Sarkozy trumpeted new and old allies, including First Lady Bernadette Chirac and Eric Besson, the former economics advisor to Royal who switched sides and gave his endorsement to Sarkozy.

Ségolène Royal had this to say to her supporters just days before the election, as quoted in the *International Herald Tribune*: "It is not the dark side that rests in us, that is sometimes being flattered here or there, it is not the dark

When a mysterious CD-ROM appeared with data accusing various French politicians of taking bribes, many people were surprised to learn of Sarkozy's possible involvement in the scandal. Thought to be incorruptible, Sarkozy was soon cleared of all suspicions regarding the situation. His political rival, Dominique de Villepin *(right)*, however, was found to be one of the organizers of the smear campaign against Sarkozy.

side that I want to awake. It is the side of light, it is the kind of hope."

She went on to say that she had heard from those "Who thought and who still think a little bit, but in the end, is it really reasonable to choose a woman? Is France going to dare? I want to say: Dare. Dare! You won't regret it."

These were two very different candidates. Alexandre Lazerges, a writer with the youth magazine *Technikart*, described them in very different terms to BBC News:

> Think of it in terms of a family. Ségolène Royal—she's like your annoying mother, telling you to clean your room but at least she'd give you some pocket money so you could go out on a Saturday night.
>
> But Sarkozy is obviously the strict father who may want what's best for you but is not able to explain it to you so you would always want to go against him. It's like the army. Don't think, just obey.

(Sarkozy's former campaign manager, Frank Tapiro, argued against this perception of Sarkozy as authoritarian by saying "when you want to change the rules you've got to be very powerful. You have sometimes to say it a little louder but that doesn't mean it's an order." He went on to say that "Many things will be corrected so that French people who didn't like him and who were maybe a little frightened of him will discover the real Nicolas Sarkozy. And I can tell you that he is a kind guy, a generous guy.")

Just days before the second round of elections, on Wednesday, May 2, the two candidates met in a nationally televised debate. For voters, it was an opportunity to see Sarkozy and Royal square off face-to-face. For the candidates, it would be an opportunity to make their positions clear and to prove to the vast viewing audience of 20 million that they were the right person to become president of France.

Sarkozy was known for his debating skills, and many expected Royal to come across as faltering and tentative against him. Instead, she appeared confident and self-assured. For many viewers, this was enough. As Sophie Miglianico said in the *International Herald Tribune*, "I was planning to vote for Ségolène and I still plan to. She defended herself well. She didn't allow herself to be crushed by Nicolas Sarkozy."

Others, though, were not convinced. If Royal's aim in the debate was to prove herself as presidential, they felt she had not quite done that. Political commentator Alain Duhamel felt that "she basically showed that she would make a formidable opposition leader."

Indeed, a number of commentators felt that Sarkozy had won the advantage over Royal. Throughout the two hour and forty minute debate, Sarkozy attempted to downplay his image as "an authoritarian with a volatile temper" and by most accounts, he succeeded.

Throughout the debate, Royal interrupted Sarkozy, climaxing in an exchange that became the most memorable and widely discussed of the debate. During an exchange on education for the disabled, Royal accused her opponent of "political immorality."

He responded by saying, "Calm down." "No, I will not calm down," she countered. "I will not calm down! I will not calm down!" Sensing an opportunity, Sarkozy went in for the kill, serenely answering back, "As president of the republic you need to be calm." This answer appeared to many to squash Royal's chances of winning the presidency.

WINNING IT ALL

Election day was Sunday, May 6, 2007. By 6:15 that evening, news sources were declaring Nicolas Sarkozy the victor; Ségolène Royal conceded defeat later that evening. By the time the final results were tabulated, it was clear that Nicolas Sarkozy had won a decisive victory, winning 53.06 percent of the vote to Royal's 46.04 percent. The short, pudgy child of immigrants, who had not gone to the right schools, who had to, as he saw it, fight to get everything he wanted, had been elected president of France. As he told Charlie Rose in an interview several months before the election,

The difference between Ségolène Royal and myself is that she went into politics through the private office of the president of the republic. She started at the highest possible level. She worked with François Mitterrand.

I started in politics right in the back row of the darkest room, and I moved forward slowly, but surely, from the last row to the front row. And once I got to the front row, I still had to climb up on to the stage. And I only had very furthest, remote—most remote seat, and gradually, gradually I moved into the center. I had to fight to do this. I had to earn my place. And I had to prove that I was up to it.

For Nicolas Sarkozy, the election results were a moment of vindication and triumph. He had convinced the French public that he was up to the job of president. Now he would have to prove that he was worthy of their trust. The hard part was just beginning.

8

The Presidency of Nicolas Sarkozy

ON MAY 16, 2007, NICOLAS SARKOZY BECAME THE SIXTH PRESIDENT OF THE French Fifth Republic. (He is also the twenty-third president in the total history of the French Republic, but presidents of France prior to the Fifth Republic had very little political power.)

The official transfer of power from Jacques Chirac to Nicolas Sarkozy took place at 11:00 A.M. at the Elysée Palace, where Sarkozy was given the nuclear codes of the French nuclear arsenal and presented with the Grand Master's Collar, the symbol of his new function of grand master of the Legion of Honor. At that exact moment, he formally became president of France.

Leyenda, a piece by Spanish composer Isaac Albéniz was played in honor of the president's wife, Cecilia, who was Albéniz's great-granddaughter. Both Sarkozy's mother, Andree, and his father, Paul, who had spoken so disparagingly of his son's future, saying "With the name you carry and the results you obtain, you will never succeed in France," attended the ceremony, as did Sarkozy's children.

The presidential motorcade, with the president on board the Peugeot 607 Paladine, traveled from the Elysée Palace to the Champs-Elysées for a public ceremony at the Arc de Triomphe. The new president then went to the Cascade du Bois de Boulogne of Paris to pay homage to the French Resistance (those who fought against Nazi occupation during World War II), including the Communist resister Guy Môquet. There, he immediately sparked controversy by proposing that all high school students read Guy Môquet's last letter to his parents before he was executed. This was seen by many on the Left as a shallow right-wing ploy, because Guy Môquet is a left-wing hero. If that was not enough for his first day in office, that afternoon Sarkozy flew to Berlin to meet with German chancellor Angela Merkel. It was obvious that the new president was a man in a hurry to get things done.

But then, Nicolas Sarkozy is a man who has always been accused of being in a hurry, a man who is too impatient to get things done, a man whose impatience makes him dangerous. Sarkozy discussed this perception of him in an interview with Charlie Rose:

> Impatient? Well, you know, I've heard so many people saying to me, Nicolas, it's too early. And then the very same said to me one day, Nicolas, it's too late. I never listened to any of them who said to me it's too soon. I always thought that the lesson of life was to do what you have to do immediately. Not tomorrow, not the day after, but right now. If that's impatience, then yes, I've been impatient. But I've been impatient to live.
>
> The most stupid thing to say is to say, I've got time. You don't have time. Time doesn't belong to you. You don't know whether you have time. . . .

Surrounded by his family, Nicolas Sarkozy *(above)* became the French president in 2007 after a ceremony marking the transfer of powers between him and former president Jacques Chirac. True to his reputation, Sarkozy immediately and energetically began to fulfill his duties as president with official meetings in Paris and Germany.

So what does it mean when people say, I have time? That is not one of the things I tend to say. Life is so precious that you have to live it. Live it from the very first second right through to the final second.

If that's impatience, then, yes, I'm impatient. But does that mean I'm dangerous? Someone who is dangerous is someone who is lying on his back. But no, I'm standing up. I want to do things. I want to shake things up. I want to modernize the country. I want to release energy. That's positive, isn't it?

So the moment that Nicolas Sarkozy became president he immediately dove into work. He was a man on a mission, a man who wanted to change France. There would be no time to waste.

THE NEW GOVERNMENT

On May 17, 2007, just one day after assuming the office of president of France, Nicolas Sarkozy appointed François Villon as prime minister, filling the office previously held by Dominique de Villepin. Sarkozy then went on to confound many of his critics who had seen him as a fervid right-winger, by appointing four of his ministers from the Left.

Perhaps the most prominent of these was his new foreign minister, Bernard Kouchner, a founder of Médecins Sans Frontières. (Médecins Sans Frontières, or Doctors Without Borders, is a humanitarian organization best known for its projects providing health care and medical training in war-torn areas and developing countries. For its efforts, the group was awarded the 1999 Nobel Peace Prize). Also appointed minister was Eric Besson, who had served as Ségolène Royal's economic advisor at the beginning of her campaign.

Sarkozy also appointed 7 women as part of a total cabinet of 15; one, Justice Minister Rachida Dati, is the first woman of northern African origin to serve in a French cabinet. Only two of Sarkozy's ministers had attended the elite Ecole National d'Administration. This school, which had educated so many of the elite that govern France, was indeed, as Tim Rice pointed out in *Prospect* magazine, "set up specifically to produce the nation's rulers. "Sarkozy, who did not attend ENA and had spent his career fighting what he saw as France's "political elite," was unlikely then to appoint them to make up his government.

One month later, on June 10 and 17, French legislative elections were held to elect the National Assembly of the Fifth Republic. Early first-round results projected a large majority for President Nicolas Sarkozy's UMP and its allies; however, second-round results showed a closer race and a stronger vote for the Left than had been anticipated. Nevertheless, the Right maintained its majority from 2002, despite, somewhat unexpectedly, losing about 40 seats to the Socialists. In the wake of these losses, there was a reshuffling of government ministers.

FOREIGN RELATIONS

One of the first major events concerning foreign relations involved the HIV trial in Libya (also known as the Bulgarian nurses' affair). In that case, six foreign workers had been accused of deliberately infecting 400 children with HIV in 1998, causing an epidemic at El-Fath Children's Hospital in Benghazi, Libya. The defendants, a Palestinian medical intern and five Bulgarian nurses, were first sentenced to death, then had their case remanded to Libya's highest court, and were then sentenced to death once again.

The epidemic at El-Fath was the first time AIDS became a public issue in Libya, and the ensuing trials were highly political and controversial. The medics insisted that they were forced to confess under torture and that they were innocent. Indeed, Saif al-Islam Gaddafi, son of Libyan leader Mu'ammar Gaddafi, later confirmed that Libyan investigators had tortured the medics with electric shocks and threatened to target their families in order to make them confess. He also confirmed that some of the children had been infected with HIV before the medics had even arrived in Libya. "There is negligence, there is a disaster that took place, there is a tragedy," he said, referring to the HIV epidemic, "but it was not deliberate."

During his investiture speech as president, Sarkozy had alluded to the case of the Bulgarian nurses, saying that France would be on their side. On July 24, 2007, Nicolas Sarkozy announced that French and European representatives had obtained the extradition of the Bulgarian nurses detained in Libya to their own country. In exchange, he signed agreements with Libya involving security, health care, and immigration, as well as a $230 million MILAN antitank missile sale.

Additionally, President Sarkozy pledged to sell Libya three civil nuclear power stations as part of a package of trade and assistance that will boost the role of French companies in the oil-rich country. This deal was criticized by the French left-wing and also by German governmental sources. Sarkozy himself denied that the arms and nuclear sales were related to the release of the nurses.

Another point of controversy involving the release of the Bulgarian nurses was the possible role played by First Lady Cecilia Sarkozy. She had gone to Libya twice in July 2007 to visit the country's leader, Colonel Mu'ammar Gaddafi, and is said to have played a prominent role in securing the Bulgarian nurses' release. There have been calls by the Left for Ms. Sarkozy to be heard by the expected parliamentary commission to investigate the terms of the release of the nurses. (As if to prove the importance of Cecilia Sarkozy's role in the release of the Bulgarian nurses, Bulgaria wanted to award her its highest state honor, but she withdrew from the trip, leaving President Sarkozy to pick up the medals alone.)

Cecilia Sarkozy proved to be a flash point of controversy throughout the first months of her husband's presidency. It has been widely reported that she did not vote during the second round of the 2007 presidential elections and did not accompany her husband when he cast his vote or during the vote count, and in fact, left for a two-week holiday in Florida directly before election day. According to rumor, she was persuaded to attend Nicolas's inauguration on the urging of her two daughters and flew in from London for the event at the last minute, dressed

One of Sarkozy's first major accomplishments as president was successfully negotiating the release of five Bulgarian nurses sentenced to death in Libya. Accused of infecting children with HIV, the nurses were allowed to return home after Sarkozy and other European officials pledged to sign military, health-care, and immigration agreements with the Libyan government. *Above*, the nurses arrive home in Sofia, Bulgaria, after almost 10 years of imprisonment in Libya.

casually in a grey sweater and white slacks—what one friend called her "escape outfit."

One month later, at the G8 Summit in June 2007, Cecilia made only a brief appearance and then left, citing an important appointment in Paris, leaving her husband as the only head of state at the dinner without a spouse in attendance. (The G8, known as the Group of Eight, is an international forum for the governments of Canada, France, Germany, Italy, Japan, Russia, the United Kingdom, and the United States.)

Then, just two months later, she once again made headlines. Nicolas had taken his family on summer vacation to the United States in August, staying with family and friends in a $30,000-a-week estate at Lake Winnipesaukee in New Hampshire. After receiving a personal invitation to dine with U.S. president George W. Bush and his family at Kennebunkport, Maine, Cecelia declined to go at the last minute, staying behind with her children in New Hampshire and leaving it to her husband to explain her absence to the Bush family.

At a news conference, President Sarkozy explained that his wife had a severe sore throat. Just one day later, however, the French newspaper *Le Parisien* reported that Cecilia was seen the day after the lunch shopping with two friends. It appeared that, based on her "rapid recovery," it was unlikely that she had truly been sick enough to stand up an invitation from President Bush. The regional daily *Charente Libre* editorialized that Cecilia's absence came close to a "diplomatic incident."

Indeed, Cecilia Sarkozy is famous for saying that "Being the First Lady, honestly, is a bore. I'm not politically correct. I don't fit the mold." By the second week of October 2007, rumors were swirling throughout France that the Sarkozys' marriage was in serious trouble. The couple had not been seen together in months, and then an announcement was made that Cecilia would not be accompanying her husband on a state visit to Morocco.

For days, there was no comment from either Nicolas or Cecilia. Then on October 19, 2007, the announcement was made. The Sarkozys' had appeared before a judge several days earlier and asked for a divorce by "mutual agreement." Cecilia told the newspaper *L'est Republicain* that it was "no longer possible" for the couple to keep their marriage together.

"I am someone who likes the shadows, serenity, tranquility," she was quoted as saying. "I had a husband who was a public man, I always knew that, I accompanied him for twenty years . . . but me, I think that is not my place. It is no longer my place.... When you marry a politician, your private life and public life become one." She called that "just the beginning of the problems."

She also expressed her frustration that her former husband had not asked her opinion when he decided that she would not testify at the parliamentary inquiry into her role in the release of the Bulgarian medical workers. "I have nothing to hide in this story," she said.

Nicolas Sarkozy himself had no immediate comment on the divorce, but his spokesman, David Martinon, insisted that the divorce would not "change anything in the functioning of the president's office. The next day though, Sarkozy had this to say to *Le Monde* when asked about his state of mind:

> My state of mind is very simple: I was elected by the French people to solve their problems, not comment on my private life, and I would have thought a major newspaper like *Le Monde* would have a greater interest in Europe than in my private life.
>
> Perhaps I should be flattered. If you think that the French people elected me for anything other than to work, work and work more—for the rest, the French ask for no comment from me. It interests them much less than you, and they are right. And perhaps they have a greater sense of propriety and more discretion, sir.

If Nicolas Sarkozy honestly thought that the French people were not interested in his private life, however, he was sadly mistaken, for the couple's divorce quickly became the talk of France and of the world. Even Libyan leader Mu'ammar Gaddafi, the man in the middle of the Bulgarian nurse controversy, expressed his shock at the Sarkozys' divorce, saying in a statement that "I deeply regret this sudden separation of my two friends. The speed with which the separation was made did not give their friends a chance to mend fences."

Curiously, even though the divorce made headlines throughout France, and it was widely discussed, the French attitude toward the divorce was one of indifference. As reported in the *New York Times*, according to a poll conducted shortly after the divorce was officially announced, 79 percent felt that it was "of little or no importance" in the country's political life. An overwhelming 92 percent said that the divorce "did not change their opinion of their president." "In France we still don't put private morality at the center of political life," said Stephane Rozes, director of CSA, the research group that took the poll. "The media and the political elite may want to hype the story . . . but the French people are more sophisticated. . . . They still profoundly believe that the private life of politicians needs to be protected."

In spite of this "sophistication," the French—and the rest of the world—became very interested in Sarkozy's private life when, one month after divorcing Cecilia, he met Carla Bruni at a dinner party. Just three months later, the couple were married at the Elysee Palace in Paris.

Marriage to Carla Bruni was guaranteed to earn the attention of the public and media alike. Bruni, a former model, singer and songwriter, had for years been a fixture of gossip columns due to her high-profile relationships with such men as musicians Mick Jagger and Eric Clapton, actor Vincent Perez, and even a former French Prime Minister, Laurent Fabius. Whether accompanying her husband on state visits, meeting with the Dalai Lama, or releasing her third album in 2008, she has been a media star, and has only increased the public's fascination with the personal life of France's very public president.

Coincidentally, on the same day that the Sarkozys' divorce was announced, France's public transportation network came to a grinding halt as public sector workers staged a series of strikes protesting Sarkozy's plan to reform the state's pension plans, ending what he saw as "special pension privileges" for more than half a million public workers. Some of Sarkozy's critics on the Left boldly accused him of timing the divorce announcement to take the media's attention away from the striking workers.

Sarkozy, though, remained confident that the public would support him rather than the strikers. Several days earlier he told a reporter, "I was elected precisely to confront difficult issues." Sarkozy's chief of staff and closest advisor, Claude Gueant, added, as quoted in the *New York Times*, "he knows that there is a great desire for change among the people. He said this throughout his campaign and that seduced public opinion. Today he is doing what he said he was going to do, and I believe that will continue to seduce."

OTHER CONTROVERSIES

The presidency of Nicolas Sarkozy got off to a fast start, with legislative accomplishments, sustained popularity in the polls, worldwide media attention, and, as described in the *New York Times*, "a flood of political and economic initiatives aimed at changing the way things are done in France." He was even named by *Vanity Fair* as one of the best-dressed men in the world. "Sarkozy for a politician is very sleek, very elegant, handsome and virile in a way that is unusual," said *Vanity Fair* special correspondent Amy Fine Collins. "He's thinking about what he's wearing and he clearly cares about it," she said. "And there's a sense of him being very comfortable in his skin and enjoying himself, and the choice of clothes reflects that."

The first months of Nicolas Sarkozy's presidency were not without controversy as well. In July 2007, Sarkozy angered many while touring in Africa. At the heart of his argument was his belief that it was important for Africans to face up to their problems, including dictatorship and widespread poverty. Calling for the same sort of "rupture" with the past as he had previously called for in France, he said, as quoted on News24, "Do you want to end the arbitrary corruption, violence . . . Do you want the rule of law? It is up to you to take the decision and if you decide so, France will be by your side like an unwavering friend."

That was all well and good, but President Sarkozy, known for his blunt talk, may have overstepped the bounds of diplomacy. Speaking in Dakar, Senegal, Sarkozy said "The African peasant only knows the eternal renewal of time, rhythmed by the end-less repetition of the same gestures and the same words. In this imaginary world where everything starts over and over again, there is no place for adventure or for the idea of progress."

He added that "France wants to help Africa to develop. But . . . there are 450 million young Africans under the age of 17, not all of them can come to Europe. And more, if we take all your doctors, all your executives, all your engineers, all your technicians, how are you going to develop your economics?"

Somewhat understandably, Alpha Oumar Konare, head of the African Union, resented Sarkozy's remarks. "This speech was not the kind of break we were hoping for," Konare told Radio France Internationale. "It was not fundamentally new, in fact it reminded us of another age, especially his comments about peasants which I did not approve of."

Within France, it was the very question of immigration that angered and divided the French people. Keeping his campaign promise, President Sarkozy began a new ministry, the Ministry of Immigration and National Identity, critics immediately attacked as being a danger to democracy.

In a petition, close to 200 historians, artists, and others from around the world demanded that the name of the min-istry be changed and that its powers be limited. The petition argued that to link immigration and the concept of national identity "is to inscribe immigration as a problem for France and the French in their very being," the petition said.

Brice Hortefeux, the head of the new ministry, now offi-cially called the Ministry of Immigration, Integration, National Identity and Co-development, introduced a bill in June 2007 that would require family members of immigrations from out-side the European Union to learn basic French before coming into the country and to become informed about French his-tory and customs. It also would require immigrants to sign a

Controversial, determined, and impervious to criticism, Nicolas Sarkozy worked and maneuvered his way to the French presidency. Though his private life sometimes garners more attention than his reforms, Sarkozy plans to revitalize the French economy, impose immigration restrictions, and encourage a stronger work ethic in the public.

contract by which they would agree to encourage the assimilation of their families into French society.

While any sort of restriction on immigration was enough to rile many on the Left, an amendment on the bill added in September of 2007 managed to infuriate many on both the Right and the Left. The amendment, as reported in the *New York Times*, "proposed the use of genetic testing to verify the bloodlines of would-be immigrants who want to join family members already living in France."

The idea was criticized by religious leaders, politicians on the Right, and also many members of Sarkozy's own party.

Fadela Amara, secretary of state for urban affairs and daughter of Algerian immigrants, threatened to resign over the proposal. "Speaking as an immigrant's daughter, I've had enough of seeing immigration exploited all the time," she told France Inter Radio. Sarkozy's response? "I am going to ask everyone to calm down."

The main argument against the amendment, as described by Elaine Sciolino in the *New York Times* is simple: French law is not based on "blood," but on recognition of a child as one's own. DNA testing for immigrants would set up a double standard, one for the French and another for the immigrant.

Of course, Nicolas Sarkozy has never been one to shy away from controversy. He said while running for president that although he supported immigration, there had to be limits and controls, and as president he has started the process to bring the immigration problem, as he sees it, under control. To his opponents, he comes across as racist, xenophobic, and willing to play on people's fear of Muslim immigrants to win support and votes.

Athough Nicolas Sarkozy has received global acclaim regarding his efforts in helping stabilize the global economy, he is still sometimes better known for the occasions when his temper gets the best of him. Case in point was an incident at the Paris International Agricultural Show on February 23, 2008. According to French media reports, Sarkozy was greeting supporters when he came across a man who refused to shake his hand. The president quickly responded "Get lost then," to which the man responded "You're making me dirty." At that point Sarkozy, a smile frozen on his face, called the man a name. The encounter struck a nerve with the French public, stirring debate over the propriety of the leader of France speaking in such terms.

To his supporters, though, he is the person they voted for: Nicolas Sarkozy, the man who promised to change France, the man who vowed to clearly break with the legacies of 1968 and reclaim France for the twenty-first century. It is a truism that you cannot make an omelet without breaking some eggs;

in other words, it is impossible to bring about change without upsetting somebody. Sarkozy, in his desire to bring about change to France, is necessarily going to face continuous opposition. It will be interesting to see how he copes and whether he will be able to make the compromises necessary to get what he wants accomplished.

Regardless of whether one supports or opposes the policies of Nicolas Sarkozy, no one can deny his patriotism and his sincere desire to make France a better country. At the conclusion of his book *Testimony*, he outlined his vision of what the new France will be. Sarkozy sees a free country, with freedom of expression, where there is no discrimination based on skin color, or name, or neighborhood, and where the right to succeed is guaranteed "to all who do what it takes." He sees a country where everyone is entitled to their beliefs and to practice their religion without being called "bigots or terrorists." He sees a France that will "be an example of modern and responsible democracy." He sees a France where "work, effort, and merit will pay off." He sees a country where public schools "will be the pillars of equal opportunity," a country that "will give more to those with greater handicaps." A country that "will lend a hand to those in a situation of need, but those in need will have to make the effort necessary to reach and hold on to that hand."

He concluded his book by writing,

> I have called this France the France of the future. In fact, it is a France that has always existed but has not always been apparent in recent years. I think there are many of us out there dreaming of such a France and wanting to create it. Yes, I am definitely French because I love our nation. I believe in its destiny. . . . To all of you, I say: anything is possible if we work together.

Nicolas Sarkozy is a man of great ambition, courage, and intelligence. It will be interesting to see if he is able to make his vision of France become a reality.

CHRONOLOGY

1955 **January 28** Nicolas Sarkozy, née Nicolas Paul
Stephane Sarkozy de Nagy-Bosca, is born in Paris,
France.

1959 Paul Sarkozy, father of Nicolas, leaves his wife and
family, forcing the family to move in with Nicolas's
grandfather, Benedict.

1975 Sarkozy gives his first major political speech at a
party meeting of the Union of Democrats for the
Republic. At the meeting he meets Jacques Chirac,
who becomes his main political mentor.

1977 Sarkozy becomes a member of the Neuilly-sur-Seine
municipal council.

1978 Sarkozy receives master's degree in private law.

1981 Sarkozy qualifies as a barrister.

1982 Sarkozy marries first wife, Marie-Dominique
Culioli.

1983 Sarkozy becomes mayor of Neuilly-sur-Seine,
beating out his local political mentor, Charles
Pasqua. He will hold the office until 2002.

1984 Meets Cecilia Maria Sara Isabel Ciganer while
marrying her to TV host Jacques Martin. He is
immediately smitten, despite the fact that she is nine
months pregnant with another man's child.

1988 Cecilia leaves her husband, Sarkozy leaves his wife,
and the couple move in together. Due to Sarkozy's
wife's reluctance to agree to a divorce, they will not
be able to marry until 1996.

1988 Sarkozy is elected to the National Assembly, the principal legislative branch of the French Parliament. He will hold his seat until 2002.

1993–1995 Sarkozy serves as minister for the budget.

1994–1995 Sarkozy serves as minister for communication.

1995 Sarkozy supports Édouard Balladur for French president in the 1995 elections rather than his mentor, Jacques Chirac. When Chirac wins the election, he turns on his protégé, and Sarkozy finds himself out of political favor.

1997 After Chirac's political party, the RPR (Rally for the Republic), loses seats in early legislative elections, Sarkozy is called in to become the party's number-two man.

1999 Sarkozy becomes head of the RPR, but after the party's poor showing in elections that year to the European Parliament, Sarkozy steps down as party leader.

2001 Sarkozy publishes political manifesto *Libre*, outlining his political beliefs.

2002–2004 Sarkozy serves as minister of the interior, internal security, and local freedoms.

2004 Faced with Sarkozy's growing popularity, Chirac moves him from minister of the interior to minister for the economy, finance, and industry, in hopes that Sarkozy will lose public favor.

2004 **November 24** Sarkozy is elected chairman of the UMP (Union for a Popular Movement), the party Chirac created to help unify France's major right-wing parties. After Chirac tells Sarkozy that he cannot be both a government minister and head of a political party, Sarkozy leaves the ministry.

2005 **June 2** After Chirac suffers a personal defeat when France votes to reject the proposed European constitution, he is forced to make major changes in his government. Sarkozy is called back to serve as minister of interior, without having to give up chairmanship of UMP.

2005 **October 27** Riots break out throughout France, caused by poverty and unemployment among young people. Sarkozy's tough response solidifies his reputation as being tough on crime and immigration.

2007 **January 14** Sarkozy is chosen by the Union for a Popular Movement to be their candidate for the office of president of France.

2007 **April 22** Sarkozy leads in the first round of elections. He will face Socialist Party candidate Ségolène Royal in the second round of elections to be held on May 6.

2007 **May 6** Sarkozy is elected as president of France, winning 53.06 percent of the vote.

2007 **May 16,** Sarkozy officially becomes the sixth president of the French Fifth Republic.

2007 **October 19** Ending weeks of speculation, Nicolas and Cecilia Sarkozy announce that they have divorced.

2007 **November 13** Nicolas Sarkozy meets former fashion model Carla Bruni at a dinner party.

2008 **February 2** Nicolas Sarkozy and Carla Bruni marry following a courtship of less than three months.

BIBLIOGRAPHY

Balmer, Crispian, and Sophie Louet. "French President Sarkozy and Wife Divorce," Reuters, October 18, 2007. Available online. URL: http://www.reuters.com/article/worldnews/idU SPAB00355520071018?feedType=RSS&feedName= worldNews.

Barratt, Nick. "Family Detective," *Telegraph*, April 14, 2007. Available online. URL: http://www.telegraph.co.uk/portal/ main.jhtml?xml=portal/2007/04/14/nosplit/ftdetective 114.xml.

Baum, Geraldine. "Sarkozy Divorce News Outweighs Strike," *Los Angeles Times*, October 19, 2007. Available online. URL: http://www.latimes.com/news/printedition/asection/la-fg-sarkozy19oct19,1,4369460.story?coll=la-news.

BBC News. "Libya 'Tortured' Bulgarian Medics." Available online. URL: http://news.bbc.co.uk/2/hi/africa/6939216.stm.

———. "Profile: Nicolas Sarkozy," May 16, 2007. Available online. URL: http://news.bbc.co.uk./go/pr/fr/-/2/hi/ europe/3673102.stm.

Beardsley, Eleanor. "French President Nicolas Sarkozy Promises Change," NPR, May 16, 2007. Available online. URL: http:// www.npr.org/templates/story/story.php?storyId=10171061.

Bell, David A. "Nicolas Sarkozy Declares an End to French Repentance," *New Republic*, July 13, 2007. Available online. URL: http://www.tnr.com/doc.mhtml?i=w070709&s= bell071307.

Bennhold, Katrin. "Sarkozy Moves Quickly to Tighten Immigration Laws," *International Herald Tribune*, June 12, 2007. Available online. URL: http://www.iht.com/articles/2007/ 06/12/frontpage/france.php.

Bennhold, Katrin, and Ariane Bernard. "Sarkozy and Royal in Homestretch," *International Herald Tribune,* May 3, 2007. Available online. URL: http://www.iht.com/bin/print.php?id=5560284.

Bernard, Ariane. "Quotes From, and About, Nicolas Sarkozy," *New York Times,* May 7, 2007. Available online. URL: http://www.nytimes.com/2007/05/07/world/europe/07/france-quotes.html.

Bitterman, Jim. "Analysis: Sarkozy Faces First Big Test," CNN. Available online. URL: http://www.cnn.com/2007/WORLD/europe/10/18/strike.analysis/.

———. "Strikes Paralyze Paris Transport," CNN. Available online. URL: http://www.cnn.com/2007/WORLD/europe/10/18/french.strikes/index.html.

Bolland, Patrick. "Guy Môquet—the Courageous Struggle," *Humanite in English,* June 1, 2007. Available online. URL: http://www.humanitieinenglish.com/article597.html.

Caldwell, Christopher. "The Man Who Would Be *le President*: Nicolas Sarkozy Wants to Wake Up France," *Weekly Standard,* March 27, 2006, Volume 011, Issue 23. Available online. URL: http://www.weeklystandard.com/Content/Public/Articles/000/000/006/7781wvxf.asp.

Campbell, Matthew. "Cecilia, You're Breaking All the Rules . . ." *Sunday Times,* July 29, 2007. Available online. URL: http://www.timesonline.co.uk/tol/news/world/europe/article2158129.ece.

Carvajal, Doreen. "A First Lady's No-show Is Seen as a No-No," *New York Times,* August 14, 2007. Available online. URL: http://www.nytimes.com/2007/08/14/world/europe/14sarkozy.html.

————. "Online Campaigning Comes into Its Own in France," *International Herald Tribune*, May 7, 2007. Available online. URL: http://www.iht.com/bin/print.php?id=5603432.

CBS News. "French President Is Best Dressed Pol," August 9, 2007. Available online. URL: http://www.cbsnews.com/stories/2007/08/08/entertainment/main3149183.shtml.

Charlton, Angela. "Sarkozy Split: She Wants 'Serenity,'" Salon.com, October 19, 2007. Available online. URL: http://www.salon.com/wires/ap/world/2007/10/19/D8SCA0800/france.sarkozy/index.html.

Cohen, Jean. "Sarkozy: 'My Roots Are in Salonika,'" European Jewish Press, April 24, 2007. Available online. URL: http://www.ejpress.org/article/16221.

Cohen, Roger. "France Must Move On," *New York Times/International Herald Tribune*, February 28, 2007. Available online. URL: http://select.nytimes.com/iht/2007/02/28/world/IHT-28globalist.html.

Cosmopolis. "Biography of Nicolas Sarkozy." Available online. URL: http://www.cosmopolis.ch/english/politics/083/nicolas_sarkozy.htm.

Crumley, Bruce. "Nicolas Sarkozy: A Grand Entrance," *Time*, September 06, 2007. Available online. URL: http://www.time.com/time/magazine/article/0,9171,901070917-1659386,00.html.

Day, Elizabeth, and Henry Samuel. "The Photographer, the Minister, His Wife, and Her 'Lover,'" *Telegraph*, August 27, 2005. Available online. URL: http://www.telegraph.co/uk/news/main.jhtml;sessionid=SNKICWLOBRPGRQ FIQMGCFFWAVCBQUIVO?xml=news/2005/08/28/wsark28.xml.

Dowd, Maureen. "Loving, Fighting, Sulking, Dancing, Betraying," Free Democracy, May 15, 2007. Available online. URL: http://freedemocracy.blogspot.com/2007/05/maureen-dowd-loving-fighting-sulking.html.

Eliaz, Raanan. "Nicolas Sarkozy, New President of France: Past and Future," European Jewish Press, May 6, 2007. Available online: URL: http://www.ejpress.org/article/16491.

———. "Sarkozy's Jewish Roots," Australian Jewish News, May 8, 2007. Available online. URL: http://www.ajn.com.au/news/news.asp?pgID=3162.

Embassy of France in Washington. "Nicolas Sarkozy: President of the Republic." Available online. URL: http://ambafrance-us.org/spip.php?article550.

EUROSOC. "Sarkozy: A New Hope?" Available online. URL: http://www.eursoc.com/news/fullstory.php/aid/172/Sarkozy:_A_New_Hope_.html.

Ganley, Elaine. "Rumors Fly in France of Sarkozy Divorce," *Boston Globe*, October 12, 2007. Available online. URL: http://www.boston.com/news/world/europe/articles/2007/10/12/rumors_fly_in_france_of_sarkozy_divorce.

Gopnik, Adam. "The Human Bomb: The Sarkozy Regime Begins." *New Yorker* (August 27, 2007): pp. 42–45.

Graff, James. "Patriot Gains," *Time*, May 10, 2007. Available online. URL: http://www.time.com/time/magazine/article/0,9171,1619141,00.html.

Henley, Jon. "Sarkozy, the Speedy Saviour," *Guardian Unlimited*, December 11, 2002. Available online. URL: http://www.guardian.co.uk/print/0,,4565624-105806,00.html.

Independent. "Cecilia Sarkozy: The First Lady Vanishes," October 2, 2007. Available online. URL: http://news.independent. co.uk/europe/article2695281.ece.

International Herald Tribune. "Critics Fear New French Ministry of Immigration and National Identity Hurts Democracy," June 22, 2007. Available online. URL: http:// www.iht.com/articles/ap/2007/06/22/europe/EU-GEN-France-Immigration-Ministry.php.

Jones, David. "Is Nicolas Sarkozy's Wife His Femme Fatale?" *Daily Mail,* May 16, 2007. Available online. URL: http://www. dailymail.co.uk/femail/article-455411/Is-Nicolas-Sarkozys-wife-femme-fatale.html.

Kedward, Rod. *France and the French: A Modern History.* Woodstock, N.Y.: Overlook Press, 2006.

King, Tim. "Nicolas Sarkozy," *Prospect Magazine,* July 2004. Available online. URL: http://www.prospect-magazine.co.uk/ article_details.php?id=6225.

Kirby, Emma-Jane. "French Confused Over the Real Sarkozy," BBC News, April 18, 2007. Available online. URL: http:// news.bbc.co.uk/go/pr/fr/-/2/hi/europe/6566649.stm.

Kramer, Jane. "Round One: The Battle for France," *New Yorker* (April 23, 2007): pp. 30–37.

Laurent, Lionel. "Has Sarkozy Rebuilt France In 100 Days?" *Forbes,* August 7, 2007. Available online. URL: http://www. forbes.com/2007/08/07/nicolas-sarkozy-france-face-markets-cx_ll_0806autofacescan02.html.

Lichfield, John. "Chirac and a Hard Place," *Bookforum,* April/ May 2007. Available online. URL: http://www.bookforum. com/inprint/014_01/192.

———. "Nicolas Sarkozy: Le Candidat," *Independent*, January 13, 2007. Available online. URL: http://news.independent. co.uk/people/profiles/article2149769.ece.

Mortkowitz, Siegfried. "Profile: Nicolas Sarkozy, France's Neo-Conservative President," EUX.TV, May 6, 2007. Available online. URL: http://eux.tv/article. aspx?articleId=7708.

New Internationalist. "Nicolas Sarkozy (Worldbeaters)" Issue 387 (March 1, 2006): p. 27.

News 24. "Sarkozy's Africa Vision Under Fire," July 28, 2007. Available online. URL: http://www.news24.com/News24/ Africa/News/0,,2-11-1447_2154961,00.html.

Ney, Catherine. *Un Pouvoir Nomme Desir.* Paris: Grasset & Fasquelle, 2007.

Paulay, Emma. "Georges Séguy: 'Sarkozy Wants to Kill Off the Spirit of Rebellion,'" *Humanite in English*, May 13, 2007. Available online. URL: http://www.humaniteinenglish.com/ article577.html.

Pedder, Sophie. "Atypically French: Sarkozy's Bid to Be a Different Kind of President," *Foreign Affairs*, May/ June 2007. Available online. URL: http://www.foreignaffairs. org/20070501fareviewessay86311/sophie-pedder/ atypically-french-sarkoqy-s-bid-to-be-a-different-kind-of-president.html?mode=print.

Reinhoudt, Jurgen. "Inside the Mind of a French Presidential Candidate," *American*, April 19, 2007. Available online. URL: http://www.american.com/archive/2007/april-0407/inside-the-mind-of-a-french-presidential-candidate.

Rose, Charlie. "A Conversation with Nicolas Sarkozy, the Interior Minister of France." *The Charlie Rose Show*, January 31, 2007.

Samuel, Henry. "Estranged Father May Have Spurred Sarkozy's Ambition," *New York Sun*, May 7, 2007. Available online. URL: http://www.nysun.com/article/53933.

———. "Sarkozy Split Fuelled by Absence from State Trip," *Telegraph*, October 16, 2007. Available online. URL: http://www.telegraph.co.uk/news/main.jhtml?xml=news/2007/10/16/wfra116.xml.

Sarkozy, Nicolas. *Testimony: France in the Twenty-first Century.* New York: Pantheon Books, 2007.

Sciolino, Elaine. "Chirac Throws His Support to Sarkozy," *International Herald Tribune*, March 21, 2007. Available online. URL: http://www.iht.com/articles/2007/03/21/news/france.php?page=1.

———. "France's Former First lady Admits Affair and Says Life in Public Eye Isn't for Her." *New York Times* (October 20, 2007): p. A5.

———. "In France, Strikes Begin as a Union Ends." *New York Times* (October 19, 2007): p. A8.

———. "Proposal in France to Test Some Immigrants' DNA," *New York Times*, October 11, 2007. Available online. URL: http://www.nytimes.com/2007/10/11/world/europe/11france.html.

———. "Sarkozy, Ever Blunt, Confounds Both Friend and Foe," *New York Times*, October 17, 2007. Available online. URL: http://www.nytimes.com/2007/10/17/world/europe/17france.html?scp=1&sq=Sarkozy%2C+Ever+Blunt%2C+Confounds+Both+Friend+and+Foe&st=nyt.

———. "Style and Vision Close Out French Campaign," *New York Times*, April 20, 2007. Available online. URL: http://www.nytimes.com/2007/04/20/world/europe/20france.html?fta=y.

Simon, Nicholas. "The Jewish Vote and the French Election,"
The Jerusalem Report, April 2, 2007. www.armeniandiaspora.
com. URL: http://www.armeniandiaspora.com/forum/
showthread.php?t=87044.

Simons, Stefan. "Sarkozy and His Model Wife," *Der
Spiegel*, Salon.com, May 28, 2007. Available online. URL:
http://www.salon.com/news/feature/2007/05/28/sarkozy/
print.html.

Smith, Craig. "Sarkozy Wins the Chance to Prove His Critics Wrong," *New York Times*, May 6, 2007. Available online.
URL: http://www.nytimes.com/2007/05/06/world/europe/
07winner.html.

———. "10 Officers Shot as Riots Worsen in French
Cities," *New York Times*, November 7, 2005. Available
online. URL: http://www.nytimes.com/2005/11/07/interna-
tional/europe/07france.html.

UnderstandFrance.org. "French Society; Politics in France;
the Right Wing and the Left Wing." Available online.
URL: http://www.understandfrance.org/France/Society.
html#ancre342516.

Vinocur, John. "Sarkozy's Ambitions Reach Wide, but
Where's the Depth?" *New York Times/International
Herald Tribune,* July 16, 2007. Available online. URL:
http://select.nytimes.com/iht/2007/07/16/world/IHT-
17politicus.html.

Willsher, Kim. "The Sarkozy Saga," *Telegraph*, February 2,
2007. Available online. URL: http://www.telegraph.co.uk/
news/main.jhtml?xml=news/2006/02/19/wsark19.xml.

Wyatt, Caroline. "Sarkozy Soap Opera Grips Paris," BBC
News, May 15, 2007. Available online. URL: http://news.
bbc.co.uk/go/pr/fr/-/2/hi/europe/6656717.stm.

Yee, April. "Sarkozy Seeks to Dodge Public Eye: Fends Off
   Press on N.H. Vacation," *Boston Globe*, August 6, 2007.
   Available online. URL: http://www.boston.com/news/local/
   new_hampshire/articles/2007/08/06/sarkozy_seeks_to_
   dodge_public_eye/?page=2.

FURTHER READING

Allport, Alan, and Arthur Meier Schlesinger. *Jacques Chirac.* New York: Chelsea House, 2007.

Gopnik, Adam. *Paris to the Moon.* New York: Random House, 2001.

Kranz, Nickie. *Teens in France* (Global Connections). Mankato, Minn.: Compass Point Books, 2007.

Moynahan, Brian. *The French Century: An Illustrated History of Modern France.* Paris: Flammarion, 2007.

Williams, Charles. *The Last Great Frenchman: A Life of General De Gaulle.* Hoboken, N.J.: Wiley, 1997.

WEB SITES

Discover France
http://www.discoverfrance.net

Understand France
http://www.understandfrance.org/index.html

PHOTO CREDITS

INDEX

About the Authors

DENNIS ABRAMS is the author of several books for Chelsea House, including biographies of Barbara Park, Anthony Horowitz, Hamid Karzai, Eminem, and Albert Pujols. He attended Antioch College, where he majored in English and communications. Abrams currently lives in Houston, Texas.

ARTHUR SCHLESINGER, JR. is remembered as the leading American historian of our time. He won the Pulitzer Prize for his books *The Age of Jackson* (1945) and *A Thousand Days* (1965), which also won the National Book Award. Schlesinger was the Albert Schweitzer Professor of the Humanities at the City University of New York and was involved in several other Chelsea House projects, including the series *Revolutionary War Leaders*, *Colonial Leaders*, and *Your Government*.